Collins

French

KS3 Revision French

KS3

Revision Guide

Karine Harrington
Steve Harrison
Sophie Jackson

Contents

	Revise	Practise	Review
KS2 Concepts			p. 20 ☐

Family and Home

	Revise	Practise	Review
Family	p. 4 ☐	p. 22 ☐	p. 42 ☐
House and Home	p. 8 ☐	p. 23 ☐	p. 43 ☐

Lifestyle

	Revise	Practise	Review
Food and Drink	p. 12 ☐	p. 24 ☐	p. 44 ☐
Sport and Health	p. 16 ☐	p. 25 ☐	p. 45 ☐

Education and Future Plans

	Revise	Practise	Review
School and Education	p. 26 ☐	p. 46 ☐	p. 66 ☐
Future Plans	p. 30 ☐	p. 47 ☐	p. 67 ☐

Leisure, Free Time and Media

	Revise	Practise	Review
Leisure	p. 34 ☐	p. 48 ☐	p. 68 ☐
TV and Technology	p. 38 ☐	p. 49 ☐	p. 69 ☐
Shopping and Money	p. 50 ☐	p. 70 ☐	p. 90 ☐

The Wider World

	Revise	Practise	Review
Where I Live	p. 54 ☐	p. 71 ☐	p. 91 ☐
Holidays	p. 58 ☐	p. 72 ☐	p. 92 ☐
Global Issues	p. 62 ☐	p. 73 ☐	p. 93 ☐

Contents

	Revise	Practise	Review

Grammar

	Revise	Practise	Review
Gender and Plurals	p. 74 ☐	p. 94 ☐	p. 108 ☐
Adjectives and Adverbs	p. 76 ☐	p. 94 ☐	p. 108 ☐
Avoir and Être	p. 78 ☐	p. 95 ☐	p. 109 ☐
ER, IR and RE Verbs	p. 80 ☐	p. 95 ☐	p. 109 ☐
Modal Verbs	p. 82 ☐	p. 96 ☐	p. 110 ☐
Faire, Aller and the Immediate Future	p. 84 ☐	p. 96 ☐	p. 110 ☐
Imperative and Reflexive Verbs	p. 86 ☐	p. 97 ☐	p. 111 ☐
Perfect Tense	p. 88 ☐	p. 97 ☐	p. 111 ☐
Future Tense	p. 98 ☐	p. 106 ☐	p. 112 ☐
Pronouns	p. 100 ☐	p. 106 ☐	p. 112 ☐
Imperfect Tense	p. 102 ☐	p. 107 ☐	p. 113 ☐
Conditional Tense and Passive Voice	p. 104 ☐	p. 107 ☐	p. 113 ☐
Mixed Test-Style Questions		p. 114 ☐	
Pronunciation Guide	p. 126		
Answers	p. 127		
Glossary	p. 137		
Index	p. 143		

Family 1

You must be able to:

- Give and ask for personal information such as name, age, birthday and nationality
- Describe your family and give personal details about members of your family, using the he / she / they forms of the verbs
- Use connectives to make longer sentences.

My Name

- **Comment t'appelles-tu?**   What are you called?
  Je m'appelle...   I am called...
- **Mon prénom c'est...**   My first name is...
  Mon nom de famille c'est...   My surname is...
- **Comment ça s'écrit?**   How do you spell it?
  Ça s'écrit...   It is spelt...

My Age

- **Quel âge as-tu?**   How old are you?
  J'ai quatorze ans.   I am fourteen years old.
  J'ai presque quinze ans.   I am nearly fifteen.
- **Quelle est la date de**   When is your birthday?
  ton anniversaire?
  Mon anniversaire c'est le   My birthday is the
  six avril.   sixth of April.
- **Tu es né(e) quand?**   When were you born?
  Je suis né(e) en deux mille un.   I was born in 2001.

> ### Key Point
>
> Remember that there are different ways to ask a question in French. For example:
>
> **Comment t'appelles-tu?**
>
> **Tu t'appelles comment?**
>
> **Comment tu t'appelles?**

Where I Live

- **Où habites-tu?**   Where do you live?
  J'habite à Bordeaux en France.   I live in Bordeaux in France.
- **Je suis anglais(e).**   I am English.
  Je suis écossais(e).   I am Scottish.
  Je suis français(e).   I am French.

Family Members

- **Dans ma famille il y a…** — In my family there are…
  personnes. — people.
- **ma mère** — my mum
  mon père — my dad
  mes parents — my parents
  ma sœur — my sister
  mon frère — my brother
  mon demi-frère — my step or half brother
  ma demi-sœur — my step or half sister
  mon beau-père — my step-dad
  ma belle-mère — my step-mum
  ma grand-mère — my grandmother
  mon grand-père — my grandad
  mon oncle — my uncle
  ma tante — my aunt
- **Je suis fille unique.** — I am an only child (for a girl).
  Je suis fils unique. — I am an only child (for a boy).
  Je n'ai pas de frères ou de sœurs. — I don't have any brothers or sisters.
- **Je suis le cadet / la cadette.** — I am the youngest.
  Je suis l'aîné(e). — I am the eldest.

Key Point

Remember not to pronounce the last consonant in words such as **comment**, **quand** and **et**.

Information about Others

- **Il s'appelle…** — He is called…
  Elle s'appelle… — She is called…
- **Il a… ans.** — He is… years old.
  Elle a… ans. — She is… years old.
- **Ils / Elles s'appellent…** — They are called…
  Ils / Elles ont… ans. — They are… years old.
- **Ma sœur s'appelle Maria et elle a douze ans.** — My sister is called Maria and she is twelve years old.
  J'ai deux frères qui s'appellent Alex et Mario et ils ont dix ans. Ils sont jumeaux. — I have two brothers who are called Alex and Mario and they are 10 years old. They are twins.

Key Vocab

je m'appelle	my name is
j'ai… ans	I am… years old
je suis	I am
je n'ai pas de	I don't have
il y a	there is / there are

> ## Quick Test
>
> 1. Say or write what your name is and how old you are in French.
> 2. Ask someone what their name is and how old they are in French.
> 3. What is the French for step-dad?
> 4. Translate into English:
>   **Bonjour! Je m'appelle Anne et j'ai presque treize ans. Mon anniversaire c'est le trente octobre. J'habite à Lille avec mes parents et mes deux frères. Mes frères s'appellent Bruno et Pierre et ils ont dix ans et sept ans.**

Family 2

You must be able to:

- Give a physical description of yourself and of other people, using adjectives
- Name pets and give a brief description, using adjectives
- Use different forms of the verbs to be and to have (**être** and **avoir**).

Describing Hair and Eyes

j'ai I have **elle / il a** she / he has **ils / elles ont** they have	**les yeux** eyes	**bleus** **verts** **noirs** **marron**	blue green black brown
	les cheveux hair	**blonds** **noirs** **bruns** **roux** **longs** **mi-longs** **courts** **raides** **frisés** **ondulés**	blonde black brown red long medium-length short straight curly wavy

> **Key Point**
>
> Adjectives agree with the noun they describe but **marron** (brown) never changes.

- **J'ai les cheveux blonds et raides. J'ai les yeux verts mais ma sœur a les yeux bleus.**
  I have blond, straight hair. I have green eyes but my sister has blue eyes.
- **Ma sœur qui a sept ans a les yeux verts et les cheveux noirs, longs et frisés.**
  My sister who is seven has green eyes and black, long, curly hair.

Describing Size

	masculine	feminine
small	**petit**	**petite**
tall	**grand**	**grande**
slim	**mince**	**mince**
big	**gros**	**grosse**

- **Je suis très grande et assez mince mais mon frère est très petit et assez gros.**
  I am very tall and quite slim but my brother is very small and quite chunky.

Describing Personality

- Here is a list of useful adjectives. Remember that with most adjectives you need to change the ending according to whether the thing or person you are describing is masculine or feminine.

	masculine	feminine
shy	timide	timide
friendly	sympa	sympa
funny	amusant	amusante
annoying	agaçant	agaçante
cute	mignon	mignonne
lazy	paresseux	paresseuse
sporty	sportif	sportive

Je suis très sympa et assez sportive, mais ma sœur est un peu paresseuse.
I am very friendly and quite sporty, but my sister is a bit lazy.

Describing Pets

- **Tu as un animal?** — Do you have a pet?
  Oui, j'ai un animal. — Yes, I have a pet.
  Non, je n'ai pas d'animaux. — No, I don't have a pet.

dog	un chien	hamster	un hamster
cat	un chat	goldfish	un poisson rouge
horse	un cheval	tortoise	une tortue
rabbit	un lapin	mouse	une souris
bird	un oiseau		

- **Chez moi, j'ai un chat et des oiseaux.** — At home I have one cat and some birds.
- To describe your pets you can use the same language as when describing people.
- **Mon chat s'appelle Léo et il a deux ans. Il est marron et il est très petit. Léo est mignon.** — My cat is called Leo and he is two years old. He is brown and he's very small. Leo is cute.

Quick Test

1. Say or write in French: I have brown eyes and long hair.
2. Choose the correct words: **Ma sœur est grande / grand.**
3. Say that you don't have a pet.
4. Choose the correct words: **Ma sœur a deux cheval / chevaux.**

House and Home 1

You must be able to:

- Say where exactly you live and the type of home you live in
- Describe your home
- Use the correct words for 'in' (**dans, à, en, au**).

Where I Live

- **Où habites-tu?**   Where do you live?
- **J'habite à...**   I live in… (name of town).
  J'habite à Londres.   I live in London.
- **J'habite en Angleterre.**   I live in England.
  en Irlande   in Ireland
  en France   in France
  au Royaume-Uni   in the United Kingdom
  au pays de Galles   in Wales
  au Sénégal   in Senegal

My Home

- **J'habite dans...**   I live in…

	une maison	a detached house
	une maison jumelée	a semi-detached house
	une ferme	a farmhouse
	un appartement	an apartment

Describing Location

- **dans une ville**   in a town / city
  dans un village   in a village
  au centre-ville   in the town centre
  à la campagne   in the countryside
  au bord de la mer   at the seaside

Key Point

The prepositions **à**, **dans**, **en** all mean 'in'. Remember that when describing where you live you need to use **à** with the town and **en** or **au** with the country.

J'habite à Bristol en Angleterre.

J'habite à Swansea au pays de Galles.

- **J'habite dans une grande maison dans une petite ville au bord de la mer.** — I live in a large house in a small town at the seaside.
- **J'habite près de Leeds.** — I live near Leeds.
  J'habite loin de Leeds. — I live far from Leeds.
  J'habite à Leeds dans le nord de l'Angleterre. — I live in Leeds in the north of England.
- **Elle habite à Marseille en France.** — She lives in Marseille in France.
- **Il habite à Dakar au Sénégal.** — He lives in Dakar in Senegal.
- **le sud** — south
  le nord — north
  l'est — east
  l'ouest — west

Inside my Home

- **Chez moi, il y a...** — At my house there is...
  la cuisine — kitchen
  la salle de bains — bathroom
  la salle à manger — dining room
  la salle de séjour — living room
  la chambre — bedroom
  la chambre de mes parents — my parents' bedroom
  la cave — cellar
  les toilettes — toilets
  le salon — living room
  le bureau — office
  le grenier — attic
  le jardin — garden
  le garage — garage
- **au premier / deuxième étage** — on the first / second floor
  au rez-de-chaussée — on the ground floor
- **Chez moi, il y a ...pièces.** — In my home there are...rooms.
- **Chez moi nous avons quatre pièces au rez-de-chaussée et cinq pièces au premier étage mais il n'y a pas de grenier.** — At my house there are four rooms on the ground floor and five rooms on the first floor but there isn't an attic.
- **Je partage ma chambre avec ma sœur.** — I share my room with my sister.

Key Point

Like all nouns in French, all rooms are either masculine or feminine. So you need to use **il** or **elle** when you refer to a room.

Ma chambre est petite et elle est bleue. My room is small and it is blue.

Key Vocab

chez	at / to someone's
il n'y a pas de	there isn't / aren't
j'habite à	I live in + town
j'habite en / au / aux	I live + country
j'habite dans	I live in + accommodation

Quick Test

1. Say that you live in a house in a town in the south of England.
2. Masculine or feminine? kitchen   bathroom   garage
3. What is the word for *far*?
4. Say that you share your bedroom with your brother.

House and Home 2

You must be able to:

- Name the pieces of furniture you have at home
- Say where things are, using prepositions
- Say what you do or don't do at home.

Items in the Home

les meubles	furniture
la chaise	chair
la table	table
l'armoire	wardrobe
la lampe	lamp
la télévision	television
l'étagère	shelf
le lit	bed
le canapé	sofa
le bureau	desk
l'ordinateur	computer
le miroir	mirror

- **Dans ma chambre j'ai une télévision mais je n'ai pas d' ordinateur. L'ordinateur est dans la chambre de mon frère.** — In my bedroom I have a television but I don't have a computer. The computer is in my brother's bedroom.

Where Things Are

- Prepositions are used to describe where things are.

dans	in
sur	on
sous	under
à côté de	near, next to
derrière	behind
devant	in front
entre	between

- **Dans ma chambre, mon ordinateur est sur mon bureau.** — In my bedroom my computer is on my desk.

Activities at Home

- **je regarde** — I watch
- **je joue** — I play
- **j'écoute** — I listen
- **je me repose** — I relax
- **je travaille** — I work
- **Je travaille dans ma chambre.** — I work in my bedroom.

> ### Key Point
>
> If the word after **à côté de** is masculine **(le)**, use **à côté du.**
>
> **Mon bureau est à côté du lit**. My desk is near the bed.
>
> Reminder: **de + le = du de + les = des**

Chores

- **Je range ma chambre.** — I tidy my room.
- **Je passe l'aspirateur.** — I do the hoovering.
- **J'aide ma mère.** — I help my mum.
- **Je fais...** — I do…
  Je fais la vaisselle. — I do the washing up.
  Je fais la cuisine. — I cook / do the cooking.
  Je fais le ménage. — I do the cleaning.
  Je fais les courses. — I do the shopping.
  Je fais mon lit. — I make my bed.

How Often?

- **rarement** — rarely
- **souvent** — often
- **tous les jours** — every day
- **quelquefois** — sometimes
- **une fois par semaine** — once a week
- **d'habitude** — usually
- **Chez moi je fais rarement la vaisselle mais je fais mon lit tous les jours.** — At home I rarely do the washing up but I make my bed every day.

Negatives

To make a sentence negative you need to use two little words that go around the verb.

- **ne...pas** — not
  Je ne fais pas mon lit. — I don't make my bed.
- **ne...jamais** — never
  Je ne fais jamais mon lit. — I never make my bed.
- **ne...rien** — nothing
  Je ne fais rien. — I do nothing.

Quick Test

1. What is the French for these items in the home: a desk, a bed, a sofa and a computer?
2. Which of the items in question 1 are masculine? Which ones are feminine?
3. Write that your bed is next to your desk.
4. Say that you help your mum every day.

Key Vocab

je fais...	I do…
je n'ai pas	I don't have
de	a / any…

Food and Drink 1

You must be able to:

- Use the French for fruits and vegetables
- Ask for drinks and snacks in a café
- Say how often you eat certain things and say what you like.

Vegetables

- **une pomme de terre**   potato
  une carotte   carrot
  un chou   cabbage
  un chou-fleur   cauliflower
  un oignon   onion
  des petits pois   peas
  des haricots verts   green beans
  un champignon   mushroom

Fruits

- **une pomme**   apple
  une poire   pear
  un citron   lemon
  une pêche   peach
  une banane   banana
  une fraise   strawberry

Ordering Drinks and Snacks

- **Je voudrais…. , s'il vous plaît.**   I'd like…, please.
  un café au lait   a white coffee
  un thé au citron   a lemon tea
  un chocolat chaud   a hot chocolate
  un coca   a coke
  une limonade   a lemonade
  une eau minérale   a mineral water
  un jus d'orange   an orange juice
  un sandwich au fromage   a cheese sandwich
  un sandwich au jambon   a ham sandwich
  un croque monsieur   typical snack of toasted cheese and ham
  une crêpe   thin pancake typical in France
  une salade niçoise   popular salad of tuna and egg that originates from Nice

Key Point

Note how to say white coffee or lemon tea in French.

un café au lait
white coffee

un thé au citron
lemon tea

The same happens with sandwich fillings:
un sandwich au fromage
a cheese sandwich

Likes and Dislikes

- **Je mange des pommes parce que j'aime le goût.** — I eat apples because I like the taste.
- **Je mange beaucoup de salade parce que c'est bon pour la santé.** — I eat lots of salad because it's good for you.
- **Je ne mange pas de champignons parce que je n'aime pas l'odeur.** — I don't eat mushrooms because I don't like the smell.
- **Je ne mange pas de fromage parce que c'est mauvais pour la santé.** — I don't eat cheese because it's bad for you.

Key Point	
Note how to say I'm hungry and I'm thirsty:	
J'ai faim.	I'm hungry.
J'ai soif.	I'm thirsty.

You use **avoir** (to have) and not **être** (to be).

How Often?

- **Je bois du café tous les jours.** — I drink coffee every day.
- **Je bois rarement du thé.** — I rarely drink tea.
- **Je mange de temps en temps des haricots verts.** — I eat green beans from time to time.
- **tous les jours** — every day
  souvent — often
  une fois par semaine — once a week
  deux fois par semaine — twice a week
  de temps en temps — from time to time
  quelquefois — sometimes
  rarement — rarely
- **En France j'aime manger un croissant tous les jours au petit déjeuner.** — In France I like to eat a croissant every day for breakfast.
- **Je ne mange jamais de frites.** — I never eat chips.

Quick Test

1. Which is the odd one out?
   a) une pomme   b) une banane
   c) un chou   d) une pêche
2. Translate the following into French: I eat apples every day.
3. Translate the following into English:
   Je n'aime pas le chou parce que le goût est horrible.
4. Which sentence is **not** true?
   a) **Les bananes sont jaunes.**
   b) **Les fraises sont rouges.**
   c) **Les petits pois sont bleus.**

Key Vocab	
je voudrais	I'd like
je mange	I eat
je bois	I drink
tous les jours	every day
souvent	often
quelquefois	sometimes
rarement	rarely
de temps en temps	from time to time

Food and Drink 2

You must be able to:

- Understand a menu
- Order a meal in a restaurant
- Follow a simple recipe.

First Course

les entrées	starters
la soupe aux légumes	vegetable soup
la salade de tomates	tomato salad
des œufs à la mayonnaise	egg mayonnaise
du pâté maison	home made pâté
du jambon	ham

Main Course

les plats principaux	mains / main courses
du poulet	chicken
du poisson	fish
du steak-frites	steak and chips
du porc	pork
de l'agneau	lamb
des fruits de mer	sea food

And Finally

les desserts	desserts / puddings
une glace	ice cream
une mousse au chocolat	chocolate mousse
la tarte au citron	lemon tart
la salade de fruits	fruit salad

Ordering a Meal

Avez-vous une table pour deux?	Do you have a table for two?
Je voudrais..., s'il vous plaît.	I'd like..., please.
Je prends...	I'll have...
Comme dessert, j'ai choisi...	For dessert, I've chosen...
La carte, s'il vous plaît.	The menu, please.
Où sont les toilettes?	Where are the toilets?
Quels légumes servez-vous?	What vegetables do you serve?
l'addition	the bill
Le service est compris.	Service is included.
un pourboire	a tip

> ### Key Point
>
> In a restaurant, you speak to the waiter or waitress using the **vous** form of the verb to be polite.
>
> **Avez-vous une table pour trois personnes?**
> Have you a table for three people?
>
> **Servez-vous...?**
> Do you serve...?

Following a Recipe

- **mettez**   put
  ajoutez   add
  versez   pour
  faites cuire   cook
  chauffez   heat up

Une Recette pour des Crêpes
A Recipe for Pancakes

- **Les ingrédients**   The ingredients
  250 grammes de farine   250 grammes of flour
  4 œufs   4 eggs
  un demi-litre de lait   half a litre of milk
  1 pincée de sel   a pinch of salt
  50 grammes de beurre   50 grammes of butter

La Méthode
Preparation

- **Mettez la farine et les œufs dans un bol.**   Put the flour and eggs into a bowl.
- **Ajoutez le lait et mélangez bien.**   Add the milk and mix well.
- **Dans une poêle chaude, mettez un peu de beurre.**   Into a hot frying pan, put a little butter.
- **Versez un peu de la pâte dans la poêle et faites cuire 1 à 2 minutes par face.**   Pour a little mixture in the pan and cook for 1 to 2 minutes each side.

Key Point

Note how to say some:

du poulet (masculine) some chicken

de la salade (feminine) some salad

des frites (plural) chips

After a quantity use **de**:
un kilo de sucre a kilo of sugar

Quick Test

1. Which is not a dessert?
   - a) une tarte aux fraises
   - b) une glace au citron
   - c) des fruits de mer
   - d) une salade de fruits
2. Translate the following into French:
   For dessert, I'll have a chocolate ice cream.
3. Translate the following into English:
   Mettez un peu de sel sur les frites.
4. Which sentence does *not* make sense?
   - a) J'ai choisi le steak parce que je suis végétarien.
   - b) J'ai choisi la salade de tomates parce que je suis végétarien.
   - c) J'ai choisi le poulet parce que je n'aime pas le steak.

Key Vocab

Avez-vous…?	Have you…?
je voudrais	I'd like
je prends	I'll have
j'ai choisi	I've chosen

Sport and Health 1

You must be able to:

* Recognise sports in French
* Talk about what sports you like
* Say how often you do sports.

Sports and Games

• **le football**	football
• **le tennis**	tennis
• **les échecs**	chess
• **le basket**	basketball
• **le badminton**	badminton
• **la pétanque**	French bowls
• **le rugby**	rugby
• **le mini-golf**	crazy golf
• **le billard**	billiards
• **le tennis de table**	table tennis
• **les jeux de société**	board games
• **les cartes**	cards

> ### Key Point
>
> When talking about sports and games **jouer** is followed by **à**:
> **jouer au football, jouer à la pétanque, jouer aux cartes.**
> But when you are talking about playing an instrument you use **jouer de**:
> **Jouer du piano, jouer de la guitare.**

Likes and Dislikes

* You already know the expressions **j'adore**, **j'aime**, **je déteste** so here are a few new phrases:

• **Je me passionne pour le foot.**	I'm crazy about football.
• **Je m'intéresse aux échecs.**	I'm interested in chess.
• **Le tennis me plaît.**	I like tennis. (Tennis pleases me.)
• **Je ne peux pas supporter le golf.**	I can't stand golf.
• **J'ai horreur du rugby.**	I really hate rugby.

How Often?

• **Je joue souvent au tennis.**	I often play tennis.
• **Je joue au hockey une fois par semaine.**	I play hockey once a week.
• **Je joue quelquefois au badminton.**	I sometimes play badminton.
• **Je ne joue jamais au tennis de table.**	I never play table tennis.

More Activities

- All these activities use the verb **faire**:

faire du vélo	to go cycling
faire de la natation	to go swimming
faire de l'équitation	to go horse-riding
faire du ski	to go skiing
faire du patinage	to go skating
faire de la gymnastique	to do gymnastics
faire de l'athlétisme	to do athletics
faire de la voile	to go sailing
faire de la planche à voile	to go wind surfing
faire une randonnée	to go walking
faire une promenade	to go for a walk
faire une promenade à vélo	to go for a bike ride

- **Ma sœur aime faire du vélo et mon frère adore faire du ski, mais moi, je me passionne pour l'équitation.** — My sister likes cycling and my brother loves skiing, but I love horse-riding.

- **En France on peut...** — In France you / one can...
  - **faire du ski à la montagne** — go skiing in the mountains
  - **faire de la natation à la plage** — go swimming at the beach

- Note this activity uses the verb **aller**: to go fishing
  aller à la pêche

Key Point

The verb **faire** is followed by **de** when talking about activities. **Faire du vélo** to go cycling (**vélo** is masculine), **faire de la natation** to go swimming (**natation** is feminine) **faire des promenades** to go for walks (**promenades** is plural).

Quick Test

1. Complete this sentence. **On peut faire de la natation...**
   a) à la gare
   b) à la banque
   c) au cinéma
   d) à la piscine
2. Translate the following into French:
   I really love football but I can't stand rugby.
3. Translate the following into English:
   Je fais souvent du vélo mais je ne joue jamais aux cartes.
4. Which is the odd one out?
   a) **les échecs**
   b) **les cartes**
   c) **le patinage**
   d) **les jeux de société**

Key Vocab

je me passionne pour...	I really love
je m'intéresse à...	I'm interested in
je ne peux pas supporter...	I can't stand
ça me plaît	I like that
j'ai horreur de...	I really hate

Sport and Health 2

You must be able to:

- Say how you are feeling
- Talk about what is good and bad for you
- Talk about how you will stay healthy in the future.

Feeling Unwell

• **Je suis malade.**	I'm ill.
• **Je suis enrhumé(e).**	I've got a cold.
• **J'ai la grippe.**	I've got flu.
• **J'ai mal à la tête.**	I've got a headache.
• **J'ai mal à la gorge.**	I've got a sore throat.
• **J'ai mal à l'estomac.**	I've got stomach ache.
• **J'ai mal au dos.**	I've got a sore back.
• **J'ai mal au bras.**	I've got a sore arm.
• **J'ai mal aux oreilles.**	I've got earache.
• **J'ai mal aux dents.**	I've got toothache.
• **J'ai mal à la jambe.**	I've got a sore leg.
• **J'ai mal au pied.**	I've got a sore foot.
• **J'ai mal aux yeux.**	I've got sore eyes.

Good or Bad for You

• **C'est bon pour la santé.**	It's good for you.
• **C'est mauvais pour la santé.**	It's bad for you / your health.
• **Je ne mange pas de frites, c'est mauvais pour la santé.**	I don't eat chips, it's unhealthy.
• **Je mange souvent de la salade, c'est bon pour la santé.**	I often eat salad, it's healthy.
• **Je ne fume pas, c'est mauvais pour les poumons.**	I don't smoke, it's bad for the lungs.
• **Le sucre est mauvais pour les dents.**	Sugar is bad for your teeth.
• **Les fruits et les légumes sont bons pour le cœur.**	Fruit and vegetables are good for the heart.

Key Point

You can use **à + la**:
J'ai mal à la tête.
I've a headache.

but **à + le = au**:
J'ai mal au dos.
I've got backache.

If the word begins with a vowel, you use **à l'**:
J'ai mal à l'estomac.
I've got tummy ache.

Plural words need **aux** in front of them:
J'ai mal aux dents.
I've got toothache.

Staying Healthy

- **Je veux rester en forme.** — I want to stay fit.
- **Je vais manger mieux.** — I'm going to eat better.
- **Je ne vais jamais fumer, le sport est meilleur pour la santé.** — I'm never going to smoke, sport is better for you.
- **Je voudrais faire plus de sport.** — I'd like to do more sport.
- **moins de sucre** — less sugar

Getting Help

- **le médecin** — the doctor
- **Je vais chez le médecin.** — I'm going to the doctor's.
- **le dentiste** — the dentist
- **J'ai un rendez-vous chez le dentiste.** — I've got a dental appointment.
- **la pharmacie** — the chemist's
- **l'hôpital** — the hospital

Quick Test

1. Complete this sentence. **J'ai mal à la...**
   a) **pied**   b) **bras**   c) **gorge**   d) **dos**
2. Translate the following into French:
   I'm ill, I've got a sore throat and a headache.
3. Translate the following into English:
   Je ne mange pas trop de fromage, c'est mauvais pour la santé.
4. Which is not healthy?
   a) **Je vais manger des fruits.**   b) **Je vais jouer au foot.**
   c) **Je vais fumer des cigarettes.**   d) **Je vais faire du ski.**

Key Vocab

je suis malade	I'm ill
j'ai mal...	I've got a sore...
c'est bon pour la santé	it's healthy
c'est mauvais pour la santé	it's unhealthy
moins de	less

Review Questions

KS2 Key Concepts

1 What colour do you get when you mix two colours together? Write the French for each new colour from these combinations.

    a) **rouge + bleu** =   b) **jaune + bleu** =

    c) **blanc + noir** =   d) **blanc + rouge** =   [4]

2 Count up to twenty in French. Write the numbers down.   [20]

3 What are the seven days of the week in French? Write them down.   [7]

4 Fill in the gaps with the missing months in French.

janvier	a)	**mars**	b) ....
mai	c)	**juillet**	d) ....
septembre	e)	**novembre**	f) .... [6]

5 Write the answers to these sums:

    a) **un + un =**   b) **trois + cinq =**   c) **six + sept =**

    d) **vingt – trois =**   e) **cinq x deux =**   f) **trois x six =**

    g) **seize – deux =**   h) **dix-neuf – huit =**

    i) **quatre x deux =**   j) **treize – douze =**   [10]

6 Match up the numbers

a)	**trente**	90	
b)	**cinquante-et-un**	30	
c)	**soixante-trois**	80	
d)	**quatre-vingts**	51	
e)	**quatre-vingt-dix**	63	[5]

7 Write the following numbers in French.

    a) 35   b) 66   c) 75   d) 84   e) 99   [5]

8 Fill in the gaps with the appropriate numbers to indicate what time it is.

a) 7:00   Il est _____ heures.

b) 7:10   Il est sept heures _____

c) 11:15   Il est _____ heures et quart.

d) 9:30   Il est _____ heures et demie.

e) 2:45   Il est _____ heures moins le quart.

f) 3:55   Il est _____ heures moins cinq.   [6]

9 Write out the times. Use the examples above to help you.

a) 2:00   b) 4:10   c) 5:15

d) 10:30   e) 5:45   f) 9:50   [6]

10 Match up two halves to form a question.

a)	C'est quand		né en décembre?
b)	Deux + deux		de ton anniversaire?
c)	Qui est		en hiver?
d)	Où fait-il chaud		aujourd'hui?
e)	Comment dit-on		ça fait combien?
f)	Quelle est la date		'janvier' en anglais?

[6]

11 Read the text and find the French for each of the phrases below.

Aujourd'hui il fait très chaud à Paris et il fait 20 degrés. Il y a du soleil dans toute la France. C'est super. Il fait aussi très beau dans le sud de l'Angleterre mais il y a du vent dans le nord de l'Angleterre. En Écosse il fait mauvais. Il fait aussi mauvais en Irlande où il pleut et il fait quinze degrés. Oh là là !!!! Attention il y a aussi du brouillard!

a) it is very hot   b) it is sunny   c) it is windy

d) it is raining   e) it is 20 degrees   f) it is bad weather

g) it is foggy   [7]

Practice Questions

Family

1 Join up the questions to the appropriate answers.

a)	Comment t'appelles-tu?		Elle s'appelle Maria.
b)	Quel âge as-tu?		Oui, j'ai un chien.
c)	Tu as des frères et des sœurs?		Non, je suis fille unique.
d)	Tu as un animal?		J'ai treize ans.
e)	Comment s'appelle ta mère?		Je m'appelle Anna.

[5]

2 Fill the gaps with the words provided in the box.

une	chien	frères	ans	longs	bleus	amusants	il

a) Je m'appelle Alex et j'ai quatorze _____

b) J'ai _____ sœur et deux _____

c) J'ai les yeux _____ et les cheveux _____

d) Mes parents sont _____

e) J'ai un _____ et _____ s'appelle Juno.

[8]

3 Look at the detail cards below and write down what the people would say about themselves.

Name: Alexandre
Date of birth: 13.05.2000
Address: Montréal
Siblings: one brother
Eyes: green
Hair: short and brown
Pets: none

Name: Karima
Date of birth: 05.07.2001
Address: Marseille
Siblings: none
Eyes: brown
Hair: long and black
Pets: one dog, age 2

[14]

House and Home

1 Translate the words below into French and include the correct article: **le, la, un** or **une**.

a) the kitchen

b) the living room

c) the bedroom

d) the attic

e) the bathroom

f) a chair

g) a bed

h) a wardrobe

i) a computer

j) a desk [10]

2 Match up the two halves of the sentences below.

a)	**Dans ma chambre**		**sur mon bureau.**
b)	**La télé est**		**dans le salon.**
c)	**Je partage ma chambre**		**il y a un ordinateur.**
d)	**Il y a deux canapés**		**avec ma sœur.**

[4]

3 Fill in the gaps using the words in the box below.

sud	chambre	dans	dix	ville	il y a
ordinateur		appartement	jardin		adore

J'habite _____ **un grand** _____ **dans une petite** _____

dans le _____ **de l'Angleterre. J'** _____ **ma ville.**

Chez moi, il y a _____ **pièces mais je n'ai pas de** _____

Dans ma _____ **j'ai un** _____ **. C'est génial.**

Dans la chambre de ma sœur _____ **une console.** [10]

Practice Questions

Food and Drink

1 Clémentine is talking about what she likes and doesn't like to eat.

Write down in English *three* things that she does eat.

Je n'aime pas les légumes parce que je les trouve horribles. Je mange beaucoup de fruits surtout des pommes rouges mais je n'aime pas tellement les poires. Je mange souvent du poulet parce que c'est bon pour la santé mais je mange rarement du poisson parce que je n'aime pas l'odeur. Comme dessert j'adore les glaces mais je ne mange plus de gâteaux parce que c'est mauvais pour la santé.

[3]

2 Look at this menu and choose a starter, main course, dessert and a drink for Olivier, a vegetarian who likes fruit but wants to avoid things which are too sweet.

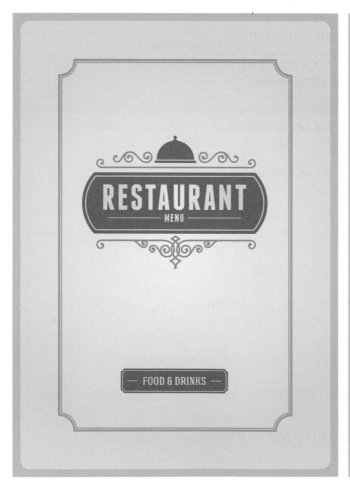

Entrées

Soupe à l'oignon
Jambon de Paris
Pâté maison

Plats principaux

Steak-frites
Côte de porc
Omelette aux champignons

Desserts

Tarte aux fraises
Glace au chocolat
Salade de fruits

Boissons

Limonade
Chocolat chaud
Thé au citron

[4]

Sport and Health

1 What problem are these people describing? Choose the correct picture.

a) J'ai mal à la tête.   b) J'ai mal au pied.   c) J'ai mal au bras.

d) J'ai mal à l'oreille.   e) J'ai mal aux yeux.

A    B    C 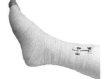   D

E    F   G

[5]

2 Identify the correct sport. Write your answer in French.

Pour faire ce sport…

a) …il faut une raquette.   b) …il faut un vélo.   c) …il faut un ballon oval.

d) …il faut un cheval.   e) …il faut des patins.   [5]

3 Put these words into two columns: **bon pour la santé** (good for you) and **mauvais pour la santé** (bad for you).

a) les frites   b) la natation   c) le sucre

d) les cigarettes   e) la salade   f) les gâteaux

g) les légumes   h) le cyclisme   [8]

School and Education 1

You must be able to:

- Say what subjects you like and dislike and why
- Describe your school
- Talk about your school day.

School and Subjects

- **l'école** — school
  le collège — French school for 11-15 year-olds
  le lycée — French school for 15-18 year-olds
- **la matière** — school subject
  l'anglais — English
  le français — French
  l'allemand — German
  l'espagnol — Spanish
  l'histoire — history
  la géographie — geography
  le dessin — art
  la musique — music
  les maths — maths
  les sciences — science
  la physique — physics
  la chimie — chemistry
  la biologie — biology
  l'informatique — IT
  la technologie — technology
  l'instruction religieuse — religious studies
  l'éducation physique et sportive (l'EPS) — PE

Key Point

You always use **le, la, l'** or **les** in front of the school subject. For example:

le français est cool;
je déteste les maths.

Likes and Dislikes

- **J'aime l'histoire.** — I like history.
- **Je n'aime pas l'anglais.** — I don't like English.
- **J'adore la chimie.** — I love chemistry.
- **Je déteste le dessin.** — I hate art.
- **Je préfère l'EPS.** — I prefer PE.
- **Ma matière préférée c'est le français.** — My favourite subject is French.

Giving Opinions

- Useful adjectives to use when saying why you like or dislike a subject:

intéressant	interesting
facile	easy
utile	useful
super	great
amusant	fun
ennuyeux	boring
difficile	difficult
inutile	useless
nul	rubbish
dur	hard

- **J'aime l'anglais parce que c'est intéressant.** — I like English because it's interesting.

- **Je n'aime pas l'informatique parce que c'est ennuyeux.** — I don't like IT because it's boring.

Giving Reasons Why

- To give reasons why you like a subject or not, you can use a phrase with a new verb in it:

  J'aime le français parce que le professeur est excellent. — I like French because the teacher is excellent.

  Je n'aime pas l'histoire parce que je ne comprends pas le professeur. — I don't like history because I don't understand the teacher.

> ### Key Point
>
> After **c'est** use the masculine form of the adjective even if you're talking about something that is feminine. For example:
>
> **J'adore la musique parce c'est intéressant**.

Quick Test

1. Which is the odd one out?
   a) le français   b) le dessin   c) la musique
2. Translate the following into French: I like geography because it is fun.
3. Translate the following into English:
   Je n'aime pas les maths parce que le professeur est nul.
4. Which sentence does *not* make sense?
   a) **J'aime le dessin, c'est nul.**
   b) **Je déteste l'EPS, c'est dur.**
   c) **J'adore les maths, c'est super.**

> ### Key Vocab
>
> | | |
> |---|---|
> | **j'adore** | I love |
> | **j'aime** | I like |
> | **je déteste** | I hate |
> | **je n'aime pas** | I don't like |
> | **parce que** | because |

School and Education 2

You must be able to:

- Talk about a typical school day
- Describe your uniform
- Talk about school rules.

The School Day

- **Je vais à l'école en bus.**   I go to school by bus.
  Je vais à l'école en voiture.   I go to school by car.
  Je vais à l'école à pied.   I go to school on foot.
- **Les cours commencent à neuf heures.**   Lessons start at 9 o'clock.
- **Il y a une récréation de quinze minutes.**   There's a 15 minute break.
- **Il y a cinq cours par jour.**   There are 5 lessons a day.
- **La pause-déjeuner est à midi.**   The lunch break is at midday.
- **Les cours finissent à quatre heures.**   Lessons finish at four o'clock.

> ### Key Point
>
> Note that the expression **il y a** means either 'there is' or 'there are'.
>
> **Il y a une cantine.**
> There's a canteen.
>
> **Il y a des laboratoires.**
> There are laboratories.

Describing your School

- **Mon école est grande / petite.**   My school is big / small.
- **Les bâtiments sont modernes.**   The buildings are modern.
  Les bâtiments sont très vieux.   The buildings are very old.
- **Il y a…**   There is / there are…
  une bibliothèque   a library
  une cantine   a canteen
  des laboratoires   laboratories
  des terrains de sport   sports fields
  mille élèves   a thousand pupils
  soixante professeurs   sixty teachers

School Rules

Revise

- Useful expressions when giving rules:

  on peut   you can
  on ne peut pas   you can't
  il est permis de   you're allowed
  il est interdit de   it is forbidden
  il faut   you must

- **Il est interdit de manger en classe.**   It is forbidden to eat in class.

- **On ne peut pas utiliser de téléphones portables.**   You can't use mobile phones.

- **Il est permis de sortir de l'école à la pause-déjeuner.**   You can leave school at lunchtime.

School Uniform

- **Mon uniforme est pratique et confortable.**   My uniform is practical and comfortable.

- **Je n'aime pas la couleur.**   I don't like the colour.

- **On doit porter...**   We must wear...
  une jupe   a skirt
  un pantalon   trousers
  des chaussures noires   black shoes
  une cravate   a tie
  une chemise blanche   a white shirt
  un blazer bleu marine   a navy blazer

- **Je voudrais aller au collège en France parce qu'il n'y a pas d'uniforme et je trouve ça super.**   I'd like to go to school in France because there's no uniform and I think that's great.

> **Key Point**
>
> When you describe uniform make sure the colour agrees.
>
> **Je porte une jupe bleue et un pullover bleu.**
> I wear a blue skirt and a blue jumper.
>
> **Il faut porter des chaussures noires.**
> You must wear black shoes.

Quick Test

1. Which is the odd one out?
   a) **on peut**   b) **il est permis**   c) **il est interdit**
2. Translate the following into French: We must wear a blue tie.
3. Translate the following into English:
   Les cours finissent à trois heures et demie.
4. Which sentence does **not** make sense?
   a) **J'aime l'uniforme, c'est horrible.**
   b) **Je déteste le blazer, ce n'est pas confortable.**
   c) **J'adore la couleur, c'est très bien.**

> **Key Words**
>
> | | |
> |---|---|
> | **Il y a** | there is / there are |
> | **Il est** | it is |
> | **interdit** | forbidden |
> | **On peut** | you can |
> | **On ne peut pas** | you can't |

Future Plans 1

You must be able to:

- Talk about jobs
- Talk about places of work
- Give opinions on work.

Jobs

- The ending of the word for some jobs changes depending on the gender it describes.

  Il est chanteur. — He is a singer.

  Elle est chanteuse. — She is a singer.

- To describe what you want to be or what you would like to be in the future use one of these phrases and add the noun for the job:

  Je veux être... — I want to be a/an…

  Je voudrais être... — I would like to be a/an…

  J'espère être... — I hope to be a/an…

  acteur / actrice — actor/actress

  avocat(e) — lawyer

  chanteur / chanteuse — singer

  chauffeur de taxi — taxi driver

  coiffeur / coiffeuse — hairdresser

  comptable — accountant

  développeur / développeuse multimédia — video game designer

  directeur / directrice de magasin — shop manager

  footballeur — footballer

  infirmier / infirmière — nurse

  ingénieur — engineer

  interprète — interpreter

  journaliste — journalist

  médecin — doctor

  pilote — pilot

  professeur — teacher

  traducteur / traductrice — translator

  vétérinaire — vet

  webdesigner — web designer

Places of Work

- **Je travaille dans...** — I work in…

  un aéroport — an airport

  un bureau — an office

  un hôpital — a hospital

un magasin	a shop
un théâtre	a theatre
une usine	a factory
une école	a school

Adjectives

- These adjectives describe personal attributes that are appropriate to the world of work.

dynamique	energetic
organisé(e)	organised
passionné(e)	passionate, keen
patient(e)	patient
poli(e)	polite
respectueux / respectueuse	respectful
tolérant(e)	tolerant
travailleur / travailleuse	hard-working

- These adjectives are useful for describing a job:

actif / active	active
bien payé(e)	well-paid
fascinant(e)	fascinating
frustrant(e)	frustrating
gratifiant(e)	rewarding
motivant(e)	motivating
stimulant(e)	stimulating

Verbs

- Use some of these together with modal verbs:

communiquer	to communicate
coopérer	to cooperate
coordonner	to coordinate
créer	to create
inventer	to invent
partager	to share
travailler seul(e) / en équipe	to work alone / in a team

- As an alternative to modal verbs use **Il faut:**

| Il faut communiquer. | You must / it is necessary to communicate. |
| Il faut être travailleur / travailleuse. | You must / it is necessary to be hard-working. |

Quick Test

1. Name three jobs that change depending on gender.
2. Where would '**un infirmier**' work?
3. Who might work '**dans un bureau**'?
4. How would you translate **Il faut partager**?

Future Plans 2

You must be able to:

- Talk about your priorities
- Use appropriate future time phrases
- Talk about future study
- Talk about ambitions.

Priorities

- Try to relate your future plans to what is important to you.

C'est essentiel.	It's essential.
C'est important.	It's important.
C'est nécessaire.	It's necessary.
Ce qui est important pour moi c'est…	What's important for me is…
ma famille	my family
ma santé	my health
mes amis	my friends
mes études	my studies
l'argent	money
le bonheur	happiness
la planète	the planet
le succès	success

Time Phrases

d'abord	first of all
après	afterwards
puis	then / next
à l'avenir	in the future
dans le futur	in the future
dans trois ans	in three years
l'année prochaine	next year
quand je quitterai le collège	when I leave school

Study

- To talk about what you are going to do, use the near future tense:

  aller + infinitive

Je vais passer mes examens.	I am going to sit my exams.
Je vais quitter le collège.	I am going to leave school.
Je vais étudier.	I am going to study.
Je vais continuer mes études.	I am going to continue my studies.
Je vais aller au lycée.	I am going to go to college/sixth form.
Je vais aller à l'université.	I am going to go to university.
Je vais faire un apprentissage.	I am going to do an apprenticeship.
Je vais chercher un emploi.	I am going to look for a job.

Reasons Why

- You can use the following phrases to describe the reasons why you will choose to study certain subjects:

Je suis fort(e) en…	I am good at…
Je suis nul(le) en…	I'm no good at…
Je suis intéressé(e) par…	I'm interested in…
Je ne suis pas intéressé(e) par…	I'm not interested in…
Je m'intéresse à…	I'm interested in…
Je ne m'intéresse plus à…	I'm no longer interested in…
J'ai une passion pour…	I have a passion for…
J'ai horreur de…	I really dislike…
Je suis accro à…	I am addicted to…

> ### Key Point
>
> The ability to move between the future tense and the near future could gain you marks in an assessment.

Ambitions

Quand j'aurai … ans …	When I am … years old…
je parlerai trois langues.	I will speak 3 languages.
je serai célèbre.	I will be famous.
je travaillerai à l'étranger.	I will work abroad.
je gagnerai beaucoup d'argent.	I will earn lots of money.
j'habiterai dans une grande maison.	I will live in a big house.
je voyagerai.	I will travel.
je ferai le tour du monde.	I will go on a world tour.
j'aiderai les autres.	I will help others.
je tomberai amoureux / amoureuse.	I will fall in love.
je me marierai.	I will get married.
j'aurai des enfants.	I will have children.
je serai heureux / heureuse.	I will be happy.

> ### Quick Test
>
> 1. Give 2 examples of ways to say you like / are good at a subject.
> 2. What are this person's priorities?
>   **'Pour moi, ma santé et l'argent sont essentiels.'**
> 3. Translate **'Je vais étudier les maths.'**
> 4. Complete this sentence **'Quand j'aurai vingt-cinq ans…'**

> ### Key Vocab
>
> | | |
> |---|---|
> | **aller** | to go |
> | **continuer** | to continue |
> | **étudier** | to study |
> | **faire** | to do |
> | **quitter** | to leave |

Leisure 1

You must be able to:

- Name musical instruments and say if you play an instrument
- Use the verb **jouer de** + instruments
- Give your opinion on music.

Music

- **les instruments de musique**   musical instruments
  le piano   piano
  le violon   violin
  le violoncelle   cello
  la clarinette   clarinet
  la trompette   trumpet
  la flûte   flute
  la guitare   guitar
  la batterie   drums

Playing an Instrument

- Use **jouer** to play, followed by the preposition **de**.
- Remember that de will need to change according to the gender of the instrument
  du   for a masculine instrument
  de la   for a feminine instrument
  de l'   for an instrument beginning with a vowel
- **Tu joues d'un instrument?**   Do you play an instrument?
- **Oui, je joue de la trompette.**   Yes, I play the trumpet.
- **Oui, je joue du piano.**   Yes, I play the piano.
- **Non, je ne joue pas d'un instrument mais je voudrais jouer du piano parce que c'est bien.**   No, I don't play an instrument but would like to play the piano because it is good.
- **Tu joues du piano?**   Do you play the piano?
  Non, je ne joue pas du piano parce que je pense que c'est difficile.   No, I don't play the piano because I think that it is difficult.

> ### Key Point
>
> For musical instruments use **jouer de**
> **je joue de la / du / de l'**
>
> For sporting activities use **jouer à**
> **je joue à la / au / à l'**

Types of Music

- **j'aime**   I like
  je préfère   I prefer
  j'adore   I love
- **Je m'intéresse à la musique.**   I am interested in music.
- **Ça me plaît.**   I like it.
- **La musique pop me plaît.**   I like pop music.
- **Le rock ne me plaît pas.**   I don't like rock and roll.
- **je n'aime pas écouter…**   I don't like to listen to…
  la musique classique   classical music
  la musique pop   pop music
  le jazz   jazz music
  le rap   rap music
  le rock   rock and roll
- **la radio**   the radio
- **mon lecteur MP3**   my MP3 player

My Favourite

- **Mon chanteur préféré c'est…**   My favourite male singer is…
- **Ma chanteuse préférée c'est…**   My favourite female singer is…
- **Mon groupe préféré c'est…**   My favourite band is…
- **Ma musique préférée c'est la musique classique parce que c'est relaxant.**   My favourite music is classical music because it is relaxing.

Adjectives

- **entraînant**   lively
- **nul**   rubbish
- **ennuyeux**   boring
- **barbant**   boring
- **relaxant**   relaxing
- **slow**   lent
- **rythmé**   rhythmic
- **fort**   loud
- **formidable**   great

Key Point

After verbs expressing likes and dislikes you need a verb in the infinitive form.
For example:

J'aime jouer

Quick Test

1. Choose the correct answer.
   Je joue de la / du trompette
   Je joue de la / du violon
2. Say what your favourite type of music is.
3. Translate
   I like to listen to classical music because it is relaxing.
4. What is the French for *'it is too slow'*?

Key Vocab

je joue de + instruments	to play an instrument
parce que	because
préféré(e)	favourite
Ça me plait	I like it

Leisure 2

You must be able to:

- Name places in town and suggest where to go
- Use **au / à la** for 'to the'/'at the'
- Make arrangements to go to the cinema.

Places in a Town

- **le restaurant** — restaurant
  le cinéma — cinema
  le supermarché — supermarket
  le centre sportif — sports centre
  le parc — park
  la patinoire — ice rink
  la piscine — swimming pool
  la bibliothèque — library
- **chez moi** — at / to my place
- **chez Sofia** — at / to Sofia's place

Key Point

au / à la / aux / à l'
all mean 'at the' and 'to the'

At and To

- If you want to say 'to the / at the', you need to use the preposition **à** followed by the article.
  à + le = au
  à + la = à la
- **Je vais à la piscine.** — I am going to the swimming pool.
- **Nous sommes au restaurant.** — We are at the restaurant.

Suggestions

- To suggest somewhere to go here are a few useful expressions:
- **On va au / à la...?**   Shall we go to the...?
- **Allons à la / au...**   Let's go to the...
- **Allons-y!**   Let's go!
- **Tu veux aller...?**   Do you want to go...?
- **On va au cinéma?**   Shall we go to the cinema?

Going to the Cinema

- **un film d'amour**   a romance film
  un film d'horreur   a horror film
  un film historique   a historical film
  un film de science-fiction   a sci-fi film
  un polar   a detective film
  un dessin animé   a cartoon
  une comédie   a comedy

Making Arrangements

- **Tu veux aller au cinéma aujourd'hui?**   Do you want to go to the cinema today?
- **Oui, bonne idée! Qu'est-ce qu'il y a?**   Yes, good idea! What is on?
- **Il y a Shrek, c'est un dessin animé.**   There is Shrek. It is a cartoon.
- **D'accord. J'adore les dessins animés. À quelle heure?**   Ok. I love cartoons. At what time?
- **Le film commence à dix heures et demie.**   The film starts at 10.30.
- **Tu veux aller au concert ce soir?**   Do you want to go to the concert tonight?

Key Point

Focus on the pronunciation of **science-fiction**, **horreur** and **historique**. 'h' is silent and 'i' is pronounced 'ee'.

Key Vocab

On va...?	Shall we go...?
aller	to go
au / à la	to / at the
chez	at / to someone's

Quick Test

1. Masculine or feminine? **cinéma / patinoire / parc / piscine**
2. Fill in with **au / à la**

   On va _____ **centre commercial?**

   Allons _____ **bibliothèque!**

   Tu veux aller _____ **restaurant?**
3. Ask someone if they want go to the swimming pool today at 10.30.
4. What is the French for 'Let's go to the cinema!'?

TV and Technology 1

You must be able to:

- Talk about which programmes you like and why
- Talk about how often you watch TV
- Use a range of adjectives and intensifiers.

TV Programmes

- **un dessin animé**   a cartoon
  un documentaire   a documentary
  un feuilleton   a soap
  un film   a film
  un jeu télévisé   a game show
  une émission de télé-réalité   a reality TV programme
  une émission de sport   a sports programme
  une émission de musique   a music programme
  une série   a series
  une comédie   a comedy
  la météo   the weather
  les infos   the news

> ### Key Point
> When preceded by a negative phrase, **un / une / des** changes to **de** (or **d'** before a vowel or a silent **h**).

Regarder (to watch)

- **Je regarde**   I watch
  Je ne regarde pas   I don't watch
  Je ne regarde jamais   I never watch
  Je ne regarde plus   I no longer watch
  Je ne regarde que   I only watch
- **Je regarde une comédie**   I watch a comedy
- **Il ne regarde pas les feuilletons.**   He doesn't watch soaps.
- **Tu ne regardes jamais les dessins animés.**   You never watch cartoons.

Likes and Dislikes

- When talking about what you like or don't like watching, you must use the infinitive.

J'aime regarder les infos.	I like watching the news.
Elle n'aime pas regarder la méteo.	She doesn't like watching the weather forecast.
Nous adorons regarder les films.	We love to watch films.

How Often?

- To say how often you do something you use an expression of frequency. Useful expressions of frequency are:

de temps en temps	from time to time
le weekend	at the weekend
parfois	sometimes
rarement	rarely
souvent	often
tous les jours	every day
une / deux fois par semaine	once / twice a week
une / deux fois par mois	once / twice a month
Je regarde de temps en temps les comédies.	I watch comedies from time to time.
Elle ne regarde pas souvent les films.	She doesn't often watch films.

Opinions

- Some useful adjectives and intensifiers when talking about TV:

amusant	entertaining	**assez**	quite
ennuyeux	boring	**très**	very
éducatif	educational	**vraiment**	really
marrant	funny	**tellement**	so
émouvant	moving	**un peu**	a bit
nul	rubbish	**trop**	too
effrayant	scary	**plutôt**	rather

Je ne regarde plus les émissions de sport une fois par semaine car elles sont vraiment nulles.	I no longer watch sport programmes once a week because they are rubbish.
Il regarde des films tous les jours même s'ils sont un peu effrayants.	He watches films every day even if they are a bit scary.

TV and Technology 2

You must be able to:

- Talk about the internet, mobile phones and video games
- Talk about social networking
- Talk about the positive and negative effects of technology.

Mobile Phones

- **J'envoie des SMS.** — I send text messages.
- **Je téléphone à mes amis.** — I phone my friends.
- **Je joue à des jeux.** — I play games.
- **Je fais des recherches en ligne.** — I do research online.

The Internet

- **Je lis des blogues.** — I read blogs.
- **Je fais des quiz.** — I do quizzes.
- **Je fais des achats en ligne.** — I do online shopping.
- **Je fais des recherches.** — I do research.
- **Je télécharge la musique.** — I download music.
- **Je tchatte sur MSN.** — I chat on MSN.
- **Je regarde des clips vidéo.** — I watch video clips.

Social Networking

- **Je poste des messages à mes copains.** — I post messages to my friends.
- **Je mets en ligne des photos.** — I upload photos.
- **Je commente des photos.** — I comment on photos.
- **J'envoie des liens vers des clips marrants.** — I send links to funny clips.
- **Je mets à jour ma page perso.** — I update my profile.
- **J'invite mes copains à des fêtes.** — I invite my friends to parties.
- **J'organise des sorties.** — I organise going out.

Video Games

- **Je joue à des jeux vidéo.** — I play video games.
- **Je joue sur l'ordinateur.** — I play on the computer.
- **Je passe des heures sur les consoles de jeux.** — I spend hours on games consoles.
- **les jeux sportifs** — sports games

- **les jeux logiques**   logic games
- **les jeux des combats**   war games
- **les jeux violents**   violent games
- **les jeux éducatifs**   educational games
- **les jeux créatifs**   creative games

Advantages of Technology

- **Ça m'aide à me détendre.**   It helps me relax.
- **C'est déstressant.**   It relieves stress.
- **On peut regarder la télé en famille.**   You can watch TV as a family.
- **C'est moins cher que sortir.**   It's less expensive than going out.
- **Ça m'aide à communiquer avec mes amis.**   It helps me to commmunicate with friends.
- **C'est plus facile de changer des projets.**   It's easier to change plans.
- **On peut communiquer plus facilement.**   You can communicate more easily.
- **On peut se tenir au courant.**   You can keep up to date.
- **Je me sens plus en sécurité.**   I feel safer.

Dangers of Technology

- **Ça rend accro.**   It's addictive.
- **On devient mollasson.**   You become a couch potato.
- **Il y a trop de violence.**   There's too much violence.
- **Il y a trop de gros mots.**   There are too many swear words.
- **On n'a pas assez d'air frais.**   You don't get enough fresh air.
- **Il y a trop de tyrans sur Internet.**   There are too many bullies online.
- **Je suis trop préoccupé.**   I am too distracted.
- **Je dépense trop d'argent chaque mois.**   I spend too much money each month.
- **C'est mauvais pour la santé.**   It's bad for your health.

> ### Key Point
>
> **On** can be translated as 'one', 'we' or 'you'. Choose whichever best fits the intended meaning of the sentence.

> ### Quick Test
>
> 1. Give two examples of things you can do on a mobile phone.
> 2. How would you translate **on peut**.
> 3. Give a disadvantage of playing video games.
> 4. Give an advantage of using the internet.

> ### Key Vocab
>
> **ça m'aide à**   it helps me to
> **on peut**   you / one can

Family

1 Who is it?

a) La mère de ma sœur, c'est ....

b) La sœur de mon père, c'est ....

c) La mère de ma mère, c'est ....

d) Le père de mon père, c'est ....

e) La sœur de mon frère, c'est .... [5]

2 Match the two halves of each sentence and translate into English.

a) J'ai les cheveux   grande et mince

b) Je suis   quatorze ans

c) J'ai   verts

d) J'ai les yeux   blonds   [8]

3 Luke is being asked about himself. Write a question for each of these answers.

a) Je m'appelle Luke.   b) J'ai 15 ans.

c) Le quinze mai.   d) Non je suis fils unique.

e) J'habite à Lille.   f) Oui, un chat, il s'appelle Pompom.   [6]

4 Fill the gaps to complete the text.

J' .... douze ans mais ma sœur .... trois ans.

J'ai les .... longs et les .... marron.

Je n'ai pas de ....

Mon chien .... Polo.   [6]

5 Translate into French:

a) I am thirteen.   b) My birthday is on the fifteenth of July.

c) I have long brown hair and green eyes.   d) I have a white cat.

e) My cat is called Fluffy.   [5]

House and Home

1 Fill in the gaps with **au, en, dans** or **à**.

a) J'habite .... Londres.

b) Nous habitons .... le nord de l'Angleterre.

c) Ma correspondante habite .... France.

d) Mes cousins habitent .... Portugal.

e) J'habite .... une grande maison. [5]

2 Put the words in the correct order

a) dans / une / maison / petite / j'habite

b) il y a / appartement / dans / pièces / cinq / mon

c) ordinateur / ma / je / pas / n' / chambre / ai / d' / dans

d) télé / sur / est / la / table / la

e) chambre / ma / petite / la / de / est / sœur [5]

3 Make these sentences negative using **ne...pas** or **ne...pas de**

a) J'ai un ordinateur dans ma chambre.

b) Ma chambre est grande.

c) Nous avons un jardin.

d) Je fais souvent la vaisselle.

e) Ma sœur a une console dans sa chambre. [5]

4 Translate into French

a) I live in a big house in the North of England.

b) At home we have ten rooms.

c) I often tidy the living room.

d) I do the washing up every day but it is very boring. [14]

Food and Drink

1 Find the fruit in each set of words.

a) une fraise   un chou   un champignon

b) un citron   une pomme de terre   des petits pois

c) un chou-fleur   une pêche   des haricots

d) une carotte   une courgette   une poire

e) un oignon   des fruits de mer   une pomme   [5]

2 Complete the sentence.

a) **Je prends la soupe** _____

     de tomates   au café   au chocolat

b) **Comme dessert j'ai choisi** _____

     une omelette   une glace   du pâté

c) **Comme boisson je prends** _____

     un jus d'orange   de la soupe   des petits pois

d) **Où sont** _____

     la table?   l'addition?   les toilettes?   [4]

3 Put the following words into one of four categories.

Viande (Meat)   **Légumes** (Vegetables)   **Desserts** (Sweets)   **Fruits** (Fruit)

a) **des champignons**   b) **des poires**

c) **une tarte aux fraises**   d) **du porc**

e) **du steak**   f) **des bananes**

g) **une glace au citron**   h) **des haricots verts**   [8]

Sport and Health

1 Catherine is talking about how often she does different sports. Put the 5 sports in order from the one she does most often to the one she never does.

a) **Je joue de temps en temps au hockey, une ou deux fois par mois.**

b) **Je fais de la natation une fois par semaine.**

c) **Je joue au basketball deux fois par semaine.**

d) **Je ne joue jamais au tennis.**

e) **Je fais du vélo tous les jours.**   [5]

2 Complete each sentence by choosing the correct ending.

a) **Je ne mange jamais de frites parce que** _____

   A j'aime le goût.   **B** c'est bon pour la santé.   **C** c'est mauvais pour la santé.

b) **Je fais souvent du sport parce que** _____

   A je veux rester en forme.   **B** c'est ennuyeux.   **C** je ne suis pas sportif.

c) **Je vais chez le dentiste parce que** _____

   A j'ai mal au pied.   **B** j'ai mal aux dents.   **C** j'ai la grippe.   [3]

3 You are giving advice on how to stay healthy. Write **il faut** or **il ne faut pas** in front of the following expressions.

a) _____ **manger de la salade.**

b) _____ **boire de l'eau.**

c) _____ **manger des biscuits.**

d) _____ **boire beaucoup de café.**

e) _____ **faire du sport.**   [5]

Practice Questions

School and Education

1 How do these people get to school? Choose the correct picture.

A

B

C

D

E

F

a) **Je vais au collège en bus.** _____

b) **Mes copines et moi, nous allons au collège à pied.** _____

c) **Je vais au collège avec ma mère. Elle m'emmène en voiture.** _____

d) **Tous les jours, je prends le train pour aller au collège.** _____ [4]

2 Choose the answer which fits best.

a) **J'adore le français parce que c'est** _____

    A difficile.   B ennuyeux.   C utile.

b) **Je n'aime pas la chimie parce que c'est** _____

    A super.   B nul.   C facile.

c) **J'aime l'histoire parce que le prof est** _____

    A ennuyeux.   B nul.   C amusant.

d) **Je déteste l'EPS parce que je suis** _____

    A nul en sport.   B fort en sport.   C sportif. [4]

Future Plans

1 Label the following pictures in French with the correct job.

a)

b)

c)

d)

[4]

2 Sort the following jobs into the correct column in the table.

coiffeur   infirmière   directeur de magasin   coiffeuse   chanteuse   directrice de magasin
avocat   infirmier   traducteur   actrice   chanteur   traductrice   avocate   acteur

Masculine	Feminine

[7]

3 Choose the correct word from below to complete the sentence.

stimulant	riche	poli

a) **Je voudrais être directeur de magasin mais il faut être** _____

b) **Je veux être pilote car ce serait** _____

c) **Je vais être footballeur car je veux être** _____   [3]

4 Describe your ambitions.

a) **Dans deux ans** _____   b) **Dans cinq ans** _____   c) **Dans dix ans** _____ [6]

Leisure

1 Fill in the gaps with the correct articles **du / de la**

a) Je joue _____ piano.

b) Mon frère joue _____ batterie.

c) Mes copines jouent _____ guitare.

d) Tu joues _____ violon?

e) Je n'aime pas jouer _____ flûte. [5]

2 Put the words in the correct order and translate in to English.

a) au / tu / restaurant / veux / aller?

b) piscine / allons / à la / demain!

c) tu / aller / avec / lundi / veux / à la / nous / soir / patinoire? [6]

3 Look at the conversation below and make two more conversations using the details provided.

Tu veux aller au cinéma aujourd'hui?

Oui, bonne idée! Qu'est-ce qu'il y a?

Il y a Shrek, c'est un dessin animé.

D'accord. J'adore les dessins animés. A quelle heure?

Le film commence à dix heures et demie.

a)
Details
When: tomorrow
Film: Batman
Type of film: a sci-fi film
Time: 4pm

b)
Details
When: Tuesday
Film: The Nativity
Type of film: a comedy
Time: 6pm

[10]

TV and Technology

1 How does **ne…jamais** affect the meaning of a sentence? [1]

2 Unjumble the words to form three sentences about things you can do online.

  a) joue des jeux je ligne à en

  b) des je recherches fais

  c) achats je en fais des ligne [3]

3 Label the parts of this sentence with the words below

Je regarde souvent des comédies car elles sont vraiment amusantes.

  a) connective

  b) opinion

  c) frequency word

  d) intensifier [4]

4 In French write two advantages of watching TV. [4]

5 In French write two disadvantages of computer games. [4]

6 Work out these frequency phrases.

  a) _ ou _ e _ t

  b) t _ _ s _ e _ _ our _

  c) _ _ a _ e _ _ nt

  d) l _ _ ee _ _ n _

  e) _ e t _ _ _ s _ n _ em _ s

  f) _ n _ f _ _ s _ a _ s _ _ _ _ n _ [6]

Shopping and Money 1

You must be able to:

- Talk about and describe clothes
- Say that you want to buy a particular item
- Describe to a shop assistant what you want.

Clothes

- **Je porte...**   I wear / I am wearing...
- **Je voudrais acheter...**   I would like to buy…
  - **un chapeau**   a hat
  - **un collant**   tights
  - **un jean**   jeans
  - **un jogging**   jogging bottoms
  - **un manteau**   a coat
  - **un pantalon**   trousers
  - **un pull**   a jumper
  - **un sweat à capuche**   a hoodie
  - **un t-shirt**   a t-shirt
  - **une chemise**   a shirt
  - **une cravate**   a tie
  - **une jupe**   a skirt
  - **une robe**   a dress
  - **une veste**   a jacket
  - **des baskets**   trainers
  - **des chaussettes**   socks
  - **des chaussures**   shoes
  - **des lunettes**   glasses

> ### Key Point
>
> Remember to check the gender of clothes as this will affect adjective agreement.
> e.g. **une chemise blanche.**

Descriptions

Most adjectives come after the noun and colours always come after the noun.

- **Il porte un jean à la mode.**   He is wearing trendy jeans.
- **Elle porte des lunettes moches.**   She is wearing ugly glasses.
- **à la mode**   fashionable / trendy
  - **à pois**   polka dotted
  - **cool**   cool
  - **démodé(e)**   old-fashioned
  - **en coton**   cotton
  - **en cuir**   leather
  - **en laine**   wool
  - **écossais(e)**   tartan
  - **moche**   ugly
  - **rayé(e)**   stripy

- A small group of adjectives always come before the noun:

un vieux pull	an old jumper
une jolie robe	a pretty dress
des belles chaussures	beautiful shoes

This and These

- To indicate a specific item or items use **ce, cet, cette** or **ces**.
- **Ce** — this (for a masculine item)
  J'aime ce chapeau. — I like this hat.
- **Cet** — this (masculine item starting with a vowel or silent 'h')
  Je voudrais cet anorak. — I would like this anorak.
- **Cette** — this (feminine)
  Je veux cette robe. — I want this dress.
- **Ces** — these
  Ces chaussures sont moches. — These shoes are ugly.

> ### Key Point
>
> All the language here can be adapted to other shopping items.
> **e.g. Je voudrais acheter un nouveau CD.**
> I'd like to buy a new CD.

Shopping

- Use pronouns to describe what you are going to buy:

Je vais acheter le t-shirt.	I am going to buy the t-shirt.
Je vais l'acheter.	I am going to buy *it*.
Je voudrais acheter les chaussettes.	I would like to buy the socks
Je voudrais les acheter.	I would like to buy *them*.

- **Est-ce que je peux vous aider?**	Can I help you?
- **Je cherche...**	I am looking for…
- **De quelle taille / couleur?**	What size / colour?
- **En...**	In…
- **Est-ce que je peux l'essayer?**	Can I try it on?
- **Ça coûte combien?**	How much does it cost?
- **Ça coûte vingt euros.**	It costs twenty euros.
Ça coûte €20.	It costs €20 (20 euros written as a symbol).
- **C'est trop cher / bon marché.**	It's too expensive / cheap.

> ### Quick Test
>
> 1. Describe what you are wearing at the moment.
> 2. Why is it important to check the gender of clothing items?
> 3. Name two adjectives that go before the noun.
> 4. Translate: I like this shirt.

Shopping and Money 2

You must be able to:

- Talk about what pocket money you receive
- Talk about what you buy with your pocket money
- Talk about household chores and jobs you do to earn money.

Pocket Money

Je reçois	I receive / get
Je reçois ... par semaine.	I receive ... per week.
Je reçois ... par mois.	I receive ... per month.
Je reçois mon argent de poche de ma mère.	I receive my pocket money from my mum.
Je ne reçois pas d'argent de poche.	I don't receive pocket money.
gagner	to earn
Je dois gagner mon argent de poche.	I have to earn my pocket money.
donner à	to give to someone
Mes parents me donnent de l'argent de poche.	My parents give me pocket money.
Son père lui donne €20.	Her dad gives her €20.
Notre grand-mère nous donne €10.	Our grandma gives us €10.

> **Key Point**
>
> When talking about what you buy with your money, use the words for some:
>
> **du / de la / de l' / des**

Saving and Spending

J'économise.	I save.
Je fais des économies pour...	I am saving for...
Je mets de l'argent de côté pour...	I put money aside for...
J'achète du maquillage.	I buy make-up.
J'achète de la nourriture au Macdo.	I buy food in McDonalds.
J'achète du crédit pour mon portable.	I buy credit for my phone.
J'achète des CD / des jeux vidéo / des billets.	I buy CDs / computer games / tickets.

Chores

Je fais les courses.	I do the shopping.
Je fais la cuisine.	I do the cooking.
Je fais la vaisselle.	I wash the dishes.
Je garde mon petit-frère.	I look after my little brother.

Je lave la voiture.	I wash the car.
Je mets la table.	I set the table.
Je passe l'aspirateur.	I do the hoovering.
Je promène le chien.	I walk the dog.
Je range ma chambre.	I tidy my bedroom.
Je sors la poubelle.	I take out the bin.
Je travaille dans le jardin.	I work in the garden.

Key Point

Time phrases

heures	o'clock
Il est six heures.	It is six o'clock.
et demie	half past
Il est six heures et demie.	It is half past six.
et quart	quarter past
moins le quart	quarter to

Part-time Jobs

J'ai un petit boulot.	I have a part-time job.
J'ai un petit job.	I have a part-time job.
Je fais du baby-sitting.	I do baby-sitting.
Je livre des journaux.	I deliver newspapers.
Je suis serveur / serveuse.	I am a waiter / waitress.
Je travaille dans une ferme.	I work on a farm.
Je travaille pour mon père.	I work for my dad.
Je travaille à la caisse.	I work at the check-out.

Describing your Job

Je commence à sept heures.	I start at seven o'clock.
Je finis à cinq heures.	I finish at five o'clock.
Je prends ma pause à une heure.	I take my break at 1 o'clock.
Je travaille 6 heures le weekend.	I work for six hours at the weekend.
Je gagne sept euros de l'heure.	I earn seven euros an hour.

Quick Test

1. What 2 chores do you do at home?
2. How much pocket money do you receive?
3. What do you do with your money?
4. Give an example of a part-time job.

Key Vocab

j'achète	I buy
je fais	I do
je reçois	I receive
je travaille	I work

Where I Live 1

You must be able to:

- Recognise places in a town
- Describe where you live and give simple directions
- Talk about the differences between the town and the country.

Places in the Town

- **la gare** — the station
- **l'hôtel de ville** — the town hall
- **le musée** — the museum
- **le jardin public** — the park
- **le centre de loisirs** — the leisure centre
- **la piscine** — the swimming pool
- **la bibliothèque** — the library
- **une église** — a church
- **une banque** — a bank
- **un centre commercial** — a shopping centre
- **le centre-ville** — the town centre
- **un magasin** — a shop
- **le marché** — the market

Where I Live

- **J'habite au centre-ville.** — I live in the town centre.
  J'habite en banlieue. — I live in the suburbs.
  J'habite dans un petit village. — I live in a small village.
  J'habite à la campagne. — I live in the countryside.

Describing a Town

- **Ma ville est...** — My town is...
  animée — lively
  propre — clean
  polluée — polluted
  bruyante — noisy
  tranquille — quiet
  ennuyeuse — boring
  industrielle — industrial

Giving Directions

- **Où est…?** — Where is…?
  Où sont…? — Where are…?
  Où est la gare, s'il vous plaît? — Where is the station, please?
  Où sont les magasins, s'il vous plaît? — Where are the shops, please?
- **Tournez à gauche.** — Turn left.
  Tournez à droite. — Turn right.
  Continuez tout droit. — Carry straight on.
  Prenez la première rue à gauche. — Take the first street on the left.
  Prenez la deuxième rue à droite. — Take the second right.

> **Key Point**
>
> **Près** means near and **loin** far away but if they come before a masculine word you use **du**:
>
> **près du parc, loin du centre-ville.**
>
> If it's feminine you say **de la**: **près de la gare, loin de la piscine.**
>
> Before plural words use **des**: **près des magasins, loin des supermarchés.**

Town or Country?

- **Je préfère habiter en ville parce que c'est animé et j'aime être près des magasins.** — I prefer living in town because it's lively and I like being near the shops.
- **Je préfère habiter à la campagne parce que c'est calme et j'aime être près de la nature.** — I prefer living in the country because it's calm and I like being near nature.
- **La ville est polluée mais la campagne est trop tranquille et c'est loin de mon école.** — The town is polluted but the country is too quiet and it's a long way from my school.

> **Quick Test**
>
> 1. Which is the odd one out?
>   a) la gare
>   b) la banque
>   c) le musée
>   d) la piscine
> 2. Translate the following into French:
>   Excuse me, where is the library, please?
> 3. Translate the following into English:
>   **Je n'aime pas la ville parce que c'est trop bruyant.**
> 4. Which phrase is describing the countryside?
>   a) **Il y a beaucoup de magasins et c'est animé.**
>   b) **Il y a beaucoup d'animaux, de fermes et d'arbres et c'est tranquille.**
>   c) **Il y a beaucoup à faire et c'est pollué.**

> **Key Vocab**
>
> | | |
> |---|---|
> | **où est…?** | where is…? |
> | **à gauche** | to the left |
> | **à droite** | to the right |
> | **tout droit** | straight on |
> | **près de** | near |
> | **loin de** | far from |

Where I Live 2

You must be able to:

- Say what there is or isn't where you live
- Talk about what you can do in your local area
- Say what improvements you would like to make in your area.

Amenities in the Town

- **il y a** — there is or there are
- **Dans ma ville, il y a...** — In my town there is...
  un cinéma — a cinema
  un théâtre — a theatre
  un musée — a museum
- **Il y a beaucoup de magasins et de restaurants mais il n'y a pas de centre de loisirs.** — There are lots of shops and restaurants but there isn't a leisure centre.
- **Il n'y a pas assez de supermarchés mais il y a un grand nombre de banques.** — There aren't enough supermarkets but there's a large number of banks.
- **La ville de Paris est très belle et il y a beaucoup d'attractions, par exemple la tour Eiffel, la cathédrale de Notre Dame et les musées.** — Paris is very beautiful and there are lots of attractions, for example the Eiffel Tower, Notre Dame cathedral and the museums.

Key Point

Notice that after a negative expression **un** and **une** change to **de**.
Il y a une piscine mais il n'y a pas de cinéma.
There is a pool but there isn't a cinema.

Things To Do

- **On peut** — you can
- **On ne peut pas** — you can't
- **Près de chez moi, on peut faire du shopping.** — Near where I live, you can go shopping.
- **On peut aller au cinéma, visiter le musée et voir un match de football.** — You can go to the cinema, visit the museum and see a football match.
- **Dans mon village, on ne peut pas faire de natation.** — In my village, you can't go swimming.
- **On ne peut pas prendre le train parce qu'il n'y a pas de gare.** — You can't catch the train because there's no station.
- **À Nice on peut aller à la plage.** — In Nice you can go to the beach.
- **À Chamonix on peut faire du ski.** — In Chamonix you can go skiing.

Improving My Town

- **Je voudrais…**
  Je voudrais créer plus de parcs.
- **Je veux…**
  Je veux voir plus de fleurs au centre-ville.
  Je veux voir moins de graffiti au centre-ville.
- **Il faut…**
  Il faut construire plus de maisons.
  Il faut nettoyer les rues au centre-ville.
  Il faut créer une nouvelle zone piétonne.
  Il faut réduire la pollution.

I would like to…
I would like to create more parks.
I want…
I want to see more flowers in the town centre.
I want to see less graffiti in the town centre.
It is necessary/we should…
We should build more houses.
It is necessary to clean the streets in the town centre.
We should create a new pedestrian zone.
We must reduce pollution.

> ### Key Point
>
> **Plus** means more and **moins** less.
>
> **Je voudrais créer plus de pistes cyclables.**
> I would like to create more cycle tracks.
>
> **À la campagne, il y a moins de pollution.**
> In the country there is less pollution.

Quick Test

1. Complete this sentence. On peut voir un film…
   - a) à la gare
   - b) à la banque
   - c) au cinéma
   - d) à la piscine
2. Translate the following into French: We should build more shops in the town centre.
3. Translate the following into English:
   Il y a trop de banques au centre-ville et il'n y a pas assez de restaurants.
4. Which phrase does not make sense?
   - a) **On peut acheter des fruits au marché.**
   - b) **On peut faire une promenade au parc.**
   - c) **On peut nager à la piscine.**
   - d) **On peut manger à la banque.**

> ### Key Vocab
>
> | | |
> |---|---|
> | **il y a** | there is |
> | **il n'y a pas** | there isn't |
> | **on peut** | you can |
> | **on ne peut pas** | you can't |
> | **il faut** | it is necessary |
> | **plus de** | more |
> | **moins de** | less |

Holidays 1

You must be able to:

- Name countries
- Describe where you usually go on holiday and give some details
- Use prepositions with countries and means of transport.

Countries

> **Key Point**
>
> Countries are either feminine or masculine so do not forget **le** or **la** in front of the countries.
>
> Most countries ending in **e** are feminine.

- Masculine Countries

le Portugal	Portugal
le pays de Galles	Wales
le Canada	Canada
le Royaume-Uni	United Kingdom
le Pakistan	Pakistan

- Feminine Countries

la France	France
la Belgique	Belgium
la Suisse	Switzerland
l'Allemagne	Germany
l'Italie	Italy
l'Irlande	Ireland
l'Angleterre	England
la Grande-Bretagne	Great Britain
l'Inde	India
les États-Unis	United States

- **J'adore le Portugal.** — I love Portugal.
- **J'aime la France.** — I like France.

Going on Holiday

- **je vais en** — I go to...+ feminine countries
  je vais au — I go to...+ masculine countries
  je vais aux — I go to...+ plural countries
- **Je vais en France pendant les vacances.** — I go to France in the holidays.
- **Où vas-tu normalement en vacances?** — Where do you usually go on holiday?
  Je vais aux Etats-Unis normalement. — I usually go to the United States.
- **Avec qui vas-tu en vacances?** — Who do you go on holiday with?
  Je vais en vacances avec mes parents et mon frère. — I go on holiday with my parents and my brother.
- **Pour combien de temps y vas-tu?** — How long do you go there for?
  J'y vais pour dix jours d'habitude. — I go there for ten days usually.

Means of Transport

- **la voiture** — car
- **la moto** — motorbike
- **le train** — train
- **l'avion** — plane
- **le bateau** — boat
- **le ferry** — ferry
- **le vélo** — bike

Key Point

The preposition **en** is used with means of transport but for on foot use **à pied**.

Travel

- **Comment vas-tu en vacances?** — How do you go on holidays?
  J'y vais en… — I go by…
  J'y vais en avion. — I go there by plane.
  On y va en train. — We go there by train.
- **On y va en train parce que c'est…** — We go by train because it is…
  rapide — fast
  confortable — comfortable
  bon marché — cheap

Useful Verbs

- To say what you are going to do on holiday use the future tense.
  j'irai — I will go
  je resterai — I will stay
  je voyagerai — I will travel
  je visiterai — I will visit
- To say what you did on holiday use the perfect tense.
  je suis allé(e) — I went
  je suis resté(e) — I stayed
  j'ai voyagé — I travelled
  j'ai visité — I visited

Quick Test

1. Which countries are feminine? **Canada**? **France**? **Espagne**? **Portugal**? **Inde**?
2. Translate into English:
   Je vais souvent aux États-Unis.
3. Fill in the gaps with the correct prepositions:
   Je vais _____ France _____ avion.
   Je suis allée _____ Portugal _____ voiture.
4. Translate into French:
   Usually I go on holiday to Italy with my parents for two weeks. I love Italy.

Key Vocab

je vais	I go
tu vas	you go
en, au, aux	to / in + countries
y	there
j'y vais	I go there

Holidays 2

You must be able to:

- Name different types of accommodation
- Mention holiday activities
- Make a reservation.

Accommodation

un hôtel	hotel
un camping	campsite
un camping-car	campervan
un appartement	flat
un gîte	typical holiday cottage in France
un complexe de vacances	holiday resort
une auberge de jeunesse	youth hostel
une colonie de vacances	holiday camp for young people, very popular in France
une colo	abbreviation of **colonie de vacances**
une tente	a tent
une caravane	caravan
chez	at someone's place
chez ma tante	at my aunt's
D'habitude je loge dans un camping.	Usually I stay in a campsite.
Je passe les grandes vacances dans une colo avec mes amis du collège.	I spend the summer holidays at a youth camp with my school friends.

Key Point

When using two verbs together the second one is always in the infinitive form.

Holiday Activities

Je vais à la plage / à la piscine.	I go to the beach / to the swimming pool.
Je me repose.	I relax.
Je me promène.	I go for a walk.
Je m'amuse.	I enjoy myself.
Je fais du sport.	I take part in sporting activities.
Je fais des courses.	I go shopping.
Je visite des monuments.	I visit monuments.
Je prends des photos.	I take photographs.
En vacances normalement je me repose beaucoup et je vais à la plage tous les jours.	On holiday I usually relax a lot and I go to the beach every day.

- **En vacances j'aime faire des courses et visiter des monuments.** On holiday I like going shopping and visiting monuments.
- **En colo il y a beaucoup d'activités.** At the youth camp there are lots of activites.

Making a Reservation

- **Je voudrais réserver…** I would like to book…
  une chambre simple a single bedroom
  une chambre double a double room
  pour deux personnes for two people
  pour deux nuits for two nights
- **avec…** with…
  un lit simple / double a single / double bed
  douche a shower
  balcon a balcony
- **sans** without
  sans salle de bains without a bathroom
- **C'est combien?** How much is it?
- **Est-ce qu'il y a…?** Is there / are there…?
  Est-ce qu'il y a un restaurant? Is there a restaurant?

Weather

- **quand / si** when / if
- **Il y a du soleil / du vent.** It is sunny / windy.
- **Il fait beau / mauvais.** The weather is good / bad.
- **Il fait froid / chaud.** It is cold / hot.
- **Il pleut / il neige.** It rains / it snows.

Making a Complaint

- **Je n'ai pas de…** I don't have a…
  Je n'ai pas de serviette. I don't have a towel.
- **cassé** broken
  Le lit est cassé. The bed is broken.
- **ne marche pas** is not working
  La télé ne marche pas. The tv is not working.
- **sale** dirty
- **bruyant** noisy

Quick Test

1. Translate into French: On holiday I stay in a caravan.
2. Translate into French: On holiday I relax and I take photos.
3. Make a reservation for a room for two people for two nights with a double bed.
4. Say the television is not working.

Global Issues 1

You must be able to:

- Use opinion phrases
- Use adverbs of quantity
- Talk about energy and environmental concerns.

Giving Opinions

• **à mon avis**	in my opinion
• **selon moi**	in my opinion
• **en ce qui me concerne**	as far as I'm concerned
• **je pense que**	I think that
• **je trouve que**	I find that
• **je crois que**	I believe that
• **je suis pour**	I am for
• **je suis contre**	I am against
• **d'un côté**	on the one hand
• **de l'autre côté**	on the other hand
• **par contre**	on the other hand

Key Point

Expressing detailed personal opinions is essential for achieving a high level. You need to be able to say what you think and give reasons why.

Adverbs of Quantity

• **assez**	enough
• **autant**	as much / as many
• **beaucoup**	a lot / many
• **moins**	less
• **peu**	few / little
• **plus**	more
• **trop**	too much / too many

The above are all followed by **de** and all other articles are omitted regardless of the gender or quantity of the noun.

• **trop *de* violence**	too much violence
• **assez *d'*argent**	enough money
• **beaucoup *de* gens**	lots of people

Dos and Don'ts

- **Il faut** you / one must, you / one need(s) to or it is neccessary to

- This is a very important and flexible phrase. It is often used to give instructions and advice. It is always followed by an infinitive.

- **Il faut prendre l'autobus.** You must take the bus.

Energy

- **Il ne faut pas...**   You must not...
  - **...détruire la couche d'ozone**   ...destroy the ozone layer
  - **...gaspiller l'énergie**   ...waste energy
  - **...laisser le robinet ouvert**   ...leave the tap running
  - **...laisser la lumière allumée**   ...leave the light on
  - **...utiliser la voiture trop souvent**   ...use the car too often
  - **...utiliser trop d'emballages**   ...use too much packaging
- **Il faut...**   You must...
  - **...baisser le chauffage**   ...turn down the heating
  - **...essayer d'utiliser des produits verts**   ...try to use green products
  - **...éteindre la lumière quand on quitte la pièce**   ...turn off the light when you leave the room
  - **...économiser l'eau**   ...save water
  - **...économiser l'énergie**   ...save energy
  - **...fermer le robinet**   ...turn off the tap
  - **...utiliser l'énergie solaire**   ...use solar energy
- As well as **il faut**, you can also use:
  - **Je dois...**   I must...
  - **On doit...**   We must / you must...

Key Point

In translation tasks always use a best fit approach. If something sounds odd when it has been translated, you probably need to re-word it to make it sound better.

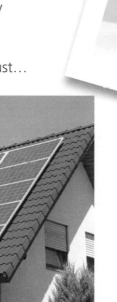

Quick Test

1. What does **il faut** mean?
2. Give two examples of an adverb of quantity.
3. When might you use the following phrases?
   d'un côté / de l'autre côté
4. Give an example of something people can do to help the environment.

Key Vocab

Il faut	you must
Il ne faut pas	you must not
à mon avis	in my opinion
selon moi	in my opinion

Global Issues 2

You must be able to:

- Talk about what concerns you
- Talk about global issues
- Talk about ways to address such issues.

Problems and Priorities

- **Ce qui me préoccupe le plus c'est…**   What worries me most is …
- **Je m'inquiète de…**   I worry about …
- **La priorité c'est...**   The priority is …
- **Le problème principal c'est…**   The main problem is …
- **Le problème le plus grave c'est…**   The most serious problem is…
- **C'est un grand problème.**   It is a big problem.
  La déforestation est un grand problème.   Deforestation is a big problem.
- **C'est un vrai souci.**   It is a real worry.
  L'effet de serre est un vrai souci.   The greenhouse effect is a real worry.

> ### Key Point
>
> Remember to turn **c'est** to **ce sont** if you are talking about 2 or more issues:
>
> **La priorité c'est**
> **Les priorités ce sont**

Current Issues

- **Les problèmes mondiaux ce sont…**   Global problems are …
  les catastrophes naturelles   natural disasters
  le changement climatique   climate change
  la conservation   conservation
  la cruauté envers les animaux   animal cruelty
  la faim   hunger
  la déforestation   deforestation
  la désertification   desertification
  l'effet de serre   the greenhouse effect
  l'énergie nucléaire   nuclear energy
  les éspèces menacées   endangered species
  la guerre   war
  les inondations   floods
  les marées noires   oil slicks
  la mondialisation   globalisation
  la pauvreté   poverty
  la pollution   pollution
  le réchauffement de la planète   global warming
  le recyclage   recycling
  le sida   aids
  la surpêche   over-fishing
  la surpopulation   over population
  le terrorisme   terrorism
  les maladies graves   serious illnesses

Addressing Problems

- **Il faut...** — One must...
- **On doit...** — One must...
- **Tout le monde doit...** — Everyone must...
  - **...acheter des produits équitables.** — ...buy fair trade products.
  - **...combattre les problèmes.** — ...fight the problems.
  - **...donner aux œuvres de bienfaisance.** — ...give to charity.
  - **...envoyer des lettres aux hommes politiques.** — ...send letters to politicians.
  - **...être conscient des autres.** — ...be concious of others.
  - **...faire quelque chose.** — ...do something.
  - **...organiser des événements.** — ...organise events.
  - **...protéger les animaux.** — ...protect animals.
  - **...recycler le verre.** — ...recycle glass.
  - **...respecter l'environnement.** — ...respect the environment.
  - **...respecter les droits des autres.** — ...respect others' rights.
  - **...sauver la planète.** — ...save the planet.
  - **...trier les déchets pour le recyclage.** — ...sort the rubbish for recycling.
  - **...utiliser les transports en commun.** — ...use public transport.

Key Point

If you are talking to a friend, use the informal imperative. **Protège! Sauve!**

The Imperative

See the grammar section on page 86 for how to form imperatives to give instructions and orders.

- **Agissez!** — Do something / take action!
- **Conservez!** — Conserve!
- **Évitez!** — Avoid!
- **Essayez!** — Try!
- **Luttez!** — Fight!
- **Jetez!** — Throw!
- **Protégez!** — Protect!
- **Recyclez!** — Recycle!
- **Réduisez!** — Reduce!
- **Respectez!** — Respect!
- **Sauvez!** — Save!
- **Soutenez!** — Support!

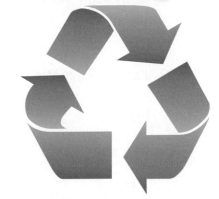

Quick Test

1. Give five examples of current global issues.
2. Translate into English:
   Je m'inquiète de.
3. What two things could you do to help save the planet?
4. Create a phrase using the imperative **respectez!**

Key Vocab

combattre	to fight
protéger	to protect
respecter	to respect
recycler	to recycle

School and Education

1 What subject are these people describing? Choose the correct picture.

A    B    C    D

E   F    G

a) **J'écris des poèmes et je lis des pièces de Shakespeare.** _____

b) **Je connais les dates des grands événements historiques.** _____

c) **Je joue de la flûte et je chante des chansons.** _____

d) **Je fais des calculs.** _____

e) **Je travaille sur l'ordinateur.** _____ [5]

2 Choose the answer which fits best.

a) **J'adore les maths parce que c'est** _____

   utile   **ennuyeux**   **nul**

b) **Je n'aime pas la musique parce que c'est** _____

   difficile   **super**   **intéressant**

c) **J'aime l'histoire parce que** _____

   le prof est ennuyeux   **le prof est désagréable**   **le prof est amusant**

d) **Je déteste l'anglais parce que c'est** _____

   utile   **ennuyeux**   **facile**   [4]

Future Plans

1 **Qui travaille dans**

   a) **un hôpital?**

   b) **un bureau?**

   c) **un magasin?**   [3]

2 What is wrong with this sentence?

   Je suis un professeur.   [1]

3 Add the most appropriate time phrase to these statements:

à l'avenir	dans deux ans	dans quatre ans

   a) _____ **je vais aller à l'université.**

   b) _____ **je vais quitter le collège.**

   c) _____ **je vais me marier.**   [3]

4 Complete the sentences with a valid reason why you will or will not study these subjects.
Look at the words in red as a clue.

   a) _____ **en anglais donc je l'étudierai au lycée.**

   b) _____ **pour le français.**

   c) _____ **par l'espagnol alors je ne le continuerai pas.**   [3]

5 Fill the gaps by choosing the correct option from below.

un bureau	motivant	développeur multimédia	dynamique	créer

   Il est _____ **et il travaille dans** _____ **. Il aime bien**

   son métier car c'est vraiment _____ **il peut** _____ **de**

   nouveaux jeux. Pour être un bon employé il doit être _____ **.**   [5]

Review Questions

Leisure

1 What are these musical instruments? Reorder the letters.

a) le o / v / l / n / o / i   b) la t / a / g / u / e / r / i   c) la e / t / b / a / t / i / e / r /

d) la p / t / e / t / e / t / m / o / r   e) le l / e / v / l / o / i / n / a / o / c / e   [5]

2 Match the two halves of each sentence.

a) | Tu joues du   jouent du piano.

b) | Ma sœur joue de la   d'un instrument?

c) | Mes frères   pas du violon.

d) | Je ne joue   guitare.

e) | Tu joues   violoncelle.   [5]

3 Fill the gaps using either **au** or **à la**.

a) On va _____ cinéma?

b) Tu veux aller _____ bibliothèque avec nous?

c) Je vais _____ patinoire tous les samedis.

d) Allons _____ centre sportif!

e) Ma sœur va souvent _____ piscine.   [5]

4 Fill in the gaps with

| préfère | préfères | préférées | préférés | préféré | préférée |

a) Ma musique _____ c'est le rap.

b) Je _____ la guitare.

c) Quelles sont tes chanteuses _____ ?

d) Qu'est-ce que tu _____ comme film?

e) Mon acteur _____ c'est Brad Pitt.

f) Quels sont tes films _____ ?   [6]

TV and Technology

1 Use a negative phrase to translate **'I no longer watch'**.   [2]

2 Copy and complete the table.

English	French
a cartoon	**un dessin animé**
a documentary	
	un jeu télévisé
a soap	
a music programme	
	une émission de télé-réalité
the weather forecast	
	les infos

[7]

3 Translate the following phrase.

I watch TV from time to time.   [2]

4 Write in French three things that you can do with a mobile phone.   [3]

5 Add a frequency word, a connective, an intensifier and an opinion to the following sentence:

Je regarde une comédie.   [3]

6 Fill in the blanks using a word from the box.

émouvante	marrantes	vraiment	éducatif

a) **La météo est** _____ **nulle.**

b) **La série est très** _____ .

c) **Le dessin animé n'est pas** _____ .   [3]

Practice Questions

Shopping and Money

1 Put these words into the correct order.

porte   **un**   **gris**   **je**   **pantalon**   [3]

2 What do you need to add, if anything, to the colours in these sentences?

e.g. Je porte une jupe noire.

a) **Je porte un pull bleu.**

b) **Je porte un pantalon blanc.**

c) **Je porte une robe vert.**

d) **Je porte une chemise jaune.**

e) **Je porte des baskets rouge.**   [5]

3 Complete this shopping dialogue.

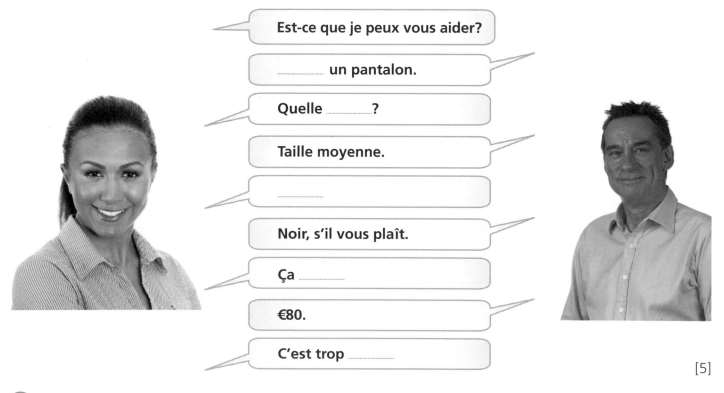

Est-ce que je peux vous aider?

.... un pantalon.

Quelle .... ?

Taille moyenne.

....

Noir, s'il vous plaît.

Ça ....

€80.

C'est trop ....

[5]

4 Rearrange the following words to create a sentence about pocket money.

44   **je**   **par**   **et**   **mois**   **reçois**

euros   **des**   **magazines**   **j'achète**   [4]

Where I live

1 Choose the correct place for these activities.

a) Je veux nager.

b) Je vais acheter des fruits et des légumes.

c) Je vais prendre le train.

d) Je voudrais faire une promenade.

e) Je veux faire du shopping.

f) Je vais changer de l'argent.

    A le centre commercial   **B** le marché   **C** la gare

    D la banque   **E** le musée   **F** le jardin public

    G la piscine   **H** la bibliothèque   [6]

2 Do these sentences describe the town (T) or the country (C)?

a) C'est calme et tranquille.

b) Il y a beaucoup de distractions, des cinémas, des théâtres, des musées.

c) L'air est sale et pollué.

d) L'air est propre et pur.

e) On peut faire des promenades dans la nature.

f) On peut aller au centre commercial.   [6]

3 Read Florence's description of her town and decide if the statements are true or false.

> Au centre-ville, il y a un centre commercial. Ici on peut acheter des vêtements. Il y a aussi une piscine et à gauche de la piscine c'est la gare. Près de la gare, il y a le jardin public où on peut se relaxer. Il y a beaucoup de restaurants et de cafés. Ma ville n'est pas très grande mais c'est animé et ce n'est jamais ennuyeux.

a) The town has a shopping centre.

b) The station is to the right of the swimming pool.

c) The park is a long way from the station.

d) There are plenty of places to eat.

e) The town is quite small.

f) Florence finds the town boring.   [6]

Practice Questions

Holidays

1 Are these countries masculine or feminine? Write the appropriate article **le, la** or **les**.

a) Belgique

b) Canada

c) France

d) Portugal

e) Espagne [5]

2 Match each place to the preposition to complete the sentences.

a) Je vais en vacances *au*   États-Unis

b) J'adore aller *en*   Paris

c) Normalement je vais en vacances *à*   Espagne

d) Mes cousins habitent *aux*   Portugal   [4]

3 Fill the gaps with words from below.

en	chaud	avion	hôtel	normalement	dans	parents	dix

_____ je vais en vacances _____ France avec mes

_____ pour _____ jours. On voyage en _____

car c'est rapide. En France, on loge dans un _____ cinq étoiles avec une

piscine et un club pour les enfants. S'il fait _____, on va à la plage

mais s'il pleut on reste _____ l'hôtel. [8]

4 Choose the appropriate form of the verb in each sentence.

a) Normalement *je vais / je suis allé(e)* en France.

b) L'année dernière *je visite / j'ai visité* la Martinique.

c) Quand je vais en France, *je loge / j'ai logé* dans un camping.

d) L'année dernière *je reste / je suis resté(e)* en France pendant dix jours. [4]

Global Issues

1. What do the following adverbs of quantity mean?

   a) moins

   b) assez

   c) trop [3]

2. Give two different ways of introducing your opinion. [2]

3. These are things you can do to help protect the environment. What do they mean?

   a) recycler le verre

   b) trier les déchets pour le recyclage

   c) utiliser les transports en commun

   d) protéger les espèces menacées

   e) combattre le réchauffement de la planète [5]

4. Write two sentences about issues to do with energy. One sentence using **il faut** to say something we must do, and one sentence using **il ne faut pas** to say something we must not do. [4]

5. Complete these opinion phrases using the words in the box.

que	suis	par	selon	côté

   a) _____ contre

   b) _____ moi

   c) de l'autre _____

   d) je _____ pour

   e) je crois _____ [5]

Gender and Plurals

You must be able to:

- Identify the correct articles for masculine or feminine words
- Make a singular word plural
- Know the words for this and these.

Genders

When you learn a French noun you also need to learn whether it is masculine or feminine.

- **un**   a (for masculine nouns)
  un chien   a dog
  un homme   a man
- **une**   a (for feminine nouns)
  une table   a table
  une femme   a woman
- **le**   the (for masculine nouns)
  le chien   the dog
- **la**   the (for feminine nouns)
  la table   the table
- **le / la** become **l'** when the following noun starts with a vowel.
  l'arbre   the tree (masculine)
  l'eau   the water (feminine)
- **le / la** also become **l'** in front of most nouns beginning with a silent 'h'*.
  l' hiver   winter
- **le / la / les / un / une / des** are called articles.
- When referring to a noun in French, you must refer to it as he / she.
  Car is feminine in French so **la voiture.**
  If I want to say that 'it is dirty', I say **'elle est sale'** (literally she is dirty).

Key Point

Masculine or feminine? Learn the gender when you learn a new word. Here are some rules that will also help.

Nouns ending in **-tion, -té, -ette, -ée, -gie, -ille** are feminine.

Nouns ending in **–isme, -eau, -age, -ment** are masculine.

There are some exceptions to the rules above.

Rules and Exceptions

- Words ending in **–isme, –ment, –age, –ean, –é** are usually masculine.
  Except:
  la plage   beach
  la page   page
  la peau   skin
- Words ending in **–té, –ée, –tion, –ence, –gie** are usually feminine.
  Except:
  le musée   museum
  le lycée   sixth form
  l'été   summer

Plurals

- To make a word plural you usually add **–s**.

un lapin	a rabbit
des lapins	rabbits
une maison	a house
des maisons	houses

Exceptions

There are a few exceptions to the general rule:

- Words ending in **–s** or **–x** do not change.

une souris	a mouse
des souris	some mice

- Words ending in **–eau** add **–x**.

un chapeau	a hat
des chapeaux	some hats

- Words in **–al** become **–aux**.

un cheval	a horse
des chevaux	some horses

> ### Key Point
>
> Pronunciation: **s** and **x** are silent at the end of the words.
>
> So **chien** and **chiens** will sound exactly the same.

This and These

The word for 'this' is:

- **ce** with a masculine word:

ce lapin	this rabbit

- **cet** with a masculine word starting with a vowel:

cet éléphant	this elephant

- **cette** with a feminine word:

cette fille	this girl

- The word for 'these' is **ces** with all plural nouns:

ces enfants	these children

> ### Quick Test
>
> 1. Write **le / la** in front of the words. Use the endings of the words to help you work out the gender.
>
>   _____ **qualité** _____ **bateau** _____ **fourchette**
>   _____ **nation**
>
> 2. Write these words in the plural.
>   **un chat   un journal   un tapis   un nez**
>
> 3. Write these words in the singular.
>   **des oiseaux   les enfants   les chiens   des bougies**

Adjectives and Adverbs

You must be able to:

- Recognise an adjective and an adverb
- Make appropriate changes to an adjective when it is feminine, feminine plural and masculine plural
- Use comparatives and superlatives to compare things, people and actions.

Adjectives

- Adjectives are words that describe nouns.
  un chat noir   a black cat
- In French, adjectives change according to the nouns they describe; singular or plural, masculine or feminine.

Basic Rules

- Add nothing for a masculine singular noun.
  un chat noir   a black cat
- Add **s** for a masculine plural noun.
- **des chat noirs**   black cats
- Add **e** for feminine singular noun.
  une table noire   a black table
- Add **es** for feminine plural nouns.
  des tables noires   black tables

Key Point

Adjectives agree with the noun they describe and usually come after the noun, except for the beauty, age, good/bad and size adjectives which can come before the noun.

Other Rules

- The feminine form of an adjective can alter depending on the ending of the adjective.

Adjective Ending	Feminine Form
–if	–ive
–eux	–euse
–er	–ère
–e or –s	do not add –e

Some Exceptions

- **blanc** (white) becomes **blanche** in the feminine form
- **vieux** (old) becomes **vieille** in the feminine form
- **beau** (handsome/beautiful) becomes **belle** in the feminine form
- **marron** (brown) does not change at all.

Adverbs

Adverbs are words that describe verbs.

- **Je marche vite.**   I walk quickly.
- **Je chante bien.**   I sing well.

To form an adverb you usually need to take the feminine form of the adjective and add **–ment**.

- **lente**   slow (feminine singular adjective)
- **lentement**   slowly (adverb)

Comparatives

To compare things or people, use:

- **plus…que**   more…than
  Je suis plus grand que mon frère.   I am taller (more tall) than my brother.
- **moins…que**   less…than
  Je suis moins sportif que mon frère.   I am less sporty than my brother.
- **aussi…que**   as…as
  Je suis aussi intelligent que mon frère. I am as intelligent as my brother.

This also can be used with adverbs:

- **Je marche plus vite que mon frère.**   I walk more quickly than my brother.

Superlatives

- **le / la / les plus**   the most
  Mon frère est le plus intelligent.   My brother is the most intelligent.
  Ma sœur est la plus intelligente.   My sister is the most intelligent.
  Mes frères sont les plus intelligents.   My brothers are the most intelligent.
- **le / la / les moins**   the least

Exceptions

- **bon**   good
  meilleur   better
  le meilleur   the best
- **mauvais**   bad
  pire   worse
  le pire   the worst

Quick Test

1. What is the feminine form for the following adjectives?
   petit   grand   rouge   gris   curieux   actif
2. Are these following words adverbs or adjectives?
   lentement   énorme   raide   librement   petit
3. Fill in the gaps:
   Elle est plus grande _____ moi.
   Je suis la _____ timide.
   Je marche _____ vite que mon père.
4. What is the French for "the best film"?

Avoir and Être

You must be able to:

- Use the correct forms of to be and to have
- Understand special uses of Avoir in French
- Identify the difference between it is / there is.

Avoir (to have)

- **j'ai**   I have
  tu as   you have (one person and informal you)

  il a   he has
  elle a   she has
  on a   one has
  nous avons   we have
  vous avez   you have (more than one person and formal you)

  ils ont   they have (all boys or boys and girls)
  elles ont   they have (all girls)

Être (to be)

- **je suis**   I am
  tu es   you are one person and informal you)

  il est   he is
  elle est   she is
  on est   one is
  nous sommes   we are
  vous êtes   you are (more than one person and formal you)

  ils sont   they are (all boys or boys and girls)
  elles sont   they are (all girls)

- **Avoir** and **être** are often used in the same way as in English.

  J'ai un chien.   I have a dog.
  Mon chien est blanc et il a de grandes oreilles.   My dog is white and it has long ears.
  Nous avons une grande maison.   We have a big house.

Special Uses of Avoir

- There are a number of phrases in which **avoir** is used in French where 'to be' is used in English.

• **avoir froid**	to be cold
J'ai froid	I am cold
• **avoir chaud**	to be hot
J'ai chaud	I am hot
• **avoir faim**	to be hungry
J'ai faim	I am hungry
• **avoir soif**	to be thirsty
J'ai soif	I am thirsty

- When talking about ages, **avoir** is used in French.

J'ai treize ans.	I am thirteen (I have thirteen years).
Quel âge as-tu?	How old are you?
Mes frères ont dix et douze ans.	My brothers are ten and twelve.

Il y a and C'est

• **il y a**	there is / are
il n'y a pas	there isn't / aren't
il y avait	there was / were
il y aura	there will be
• **c'est**	it is
ce n'est pas	it is not
c'était	it was
ce sera	it will be

> **Key Point**
>
> **Avoir** and **être** are irregular verbs.

> **Quick Test**
>
> 1. Fill in with the correct form of **être**.
>   Je _____ grande.
>   Nous _____ petits.
>   Mes cheveux _____ longs.
> 2. Fill in the with the correct form of **avoir**.
>   Elle _____ les cheveux blonds.
>   Elles _____ un chien.
>   Il _____ une voiture rouge.
> 3. Translate into French: I am 14 years old and my sister is 16 years old.
> 4. Say that you are thirsty in French.

ER, IR and RE Verbs

You must be able to:

- Recognise verbs from the main verb groups
- Use **–er**, **–ir**, and **–re** verbs accurately
- Use regular verbs in singular and plural forms.

Main Groups

- There are three main groups of verbs in French. Verbs that end in:

er	ir	re
manger to eat	**finir** to finish	**attendre** to wait

- These verbs are called **-er** verbs, **-ir** verbs and **-re** verbs. They are also called regular verbs.

Chanter (to sing)

- **je chante**   I sing or I am singing
  tu chantes   you sing or you are singing
  il / elle / on chante   he / she / one sings / is singing
  nous chantons   we sing / we are singing
  vous chantez   you sing / you are singing
  ils / elles chantent   they sing / they are singing

Common –er Verbs

- **aimer**   to like
- **détester**   to hate
- **regarder**   to watch
- **préférer**   to prefer
- **acheter**   to buy
- **visiter**   to visit
- **habiter**   to live
- **adorer**   to love
- **travailler**   to work
- **jouer**   to play

Finir (to finish)

- **je finis** — I finish / I am finishing
  tu finis — you finish / you are finishing
  il / elle finit — he / she finishes / he / she is finishing
  nous finissons — we finish / we are finishing
  vous finissez — you finish / you are finishing
  ils / elles finissent — they finish / they are finishing

Common –ir Verbs

- **choisir** — to choose
- **rougir** — to blush
- **remplir** — to fill
- The following –ir verbs are irregular:
  dormir — to sleep
  sortir — to go out
  partir — to leave
- They are irregular as their stems change. The endings are **–s,-s,-t,-ons,-ez,-ent.**
  Je dors — I sleep / I am sleeping
  Nous dormons — We sleep / We are sleeping
  Je sors — I go out / I am going out
  Nous sortons — We go out / We are going out

Attendre (to wait)

- **j'attends** — I wait / I am waiting
  tu attends — you wait / you are waiting
  il / elle attend — he / she waits / is waiting
  nous attendons — we wait / we are waiting
  vous attendez — you wait / you are waiting
  ils / elles attendent — they wait / they are waiting

Common –re verbs

- **perdre** — to lose
- **vendre** — to sell
- **entendre** — to hear
- **répondre** — to answer

Quick Test

1. Add the correct endings of the verbs in the present tense.
   je regard   il fini   nous entend   ils travaill
2. Translate the following verbs into French:
   I hear   she loves   we answer   we choose
3. Translate the following verbs into French:
   I am playing   she is waiting   they are watching   he is singing
4. What is the English for **je joue?**

Modal Verbs

You must be able to:

- Form modal verbs correctly
- Use them with infinitives of other verbs
- Use the negative form.

Modal Verbs

- Modal verbs are very useful. They are followed by the infinitive (the form you find in the dictionary) of another verb.

Vouloir (to want to)

- **je veux...**   I want to...
  tu veux...   you want to...
  il / elle / on veut...   he / she / one wants to...
  nous voulons...   we want to...
  vous voulez...   you want to...
  ils / elles veulent...   they want to...
- **Je veux faire mes devoirs.**   I want to do my homework.
  Tu veux jouer au foot?   Do you want to play football?
  Elle veut manger à la cantine.   She wants to eat in the canteen.
  Elles veulent porter un pantalon. They want to wear trousers.

Pouvoir (to be able to / can)

- **je peux...**   I can...
  tu peux...   you can...
  il / elle / on peut...   he / she / one can...
  nous pouvons...   we can...
  vous pouvez...   you can...
  ils / elles peuvent...   they can...
- **Je peux aller aux toilettes?**   Can I go to the toilet?
  Tu peux m'aider?   Can you help me?
  Elle peut finir son travail.   She can finish her work.
  Elle peuvent ouvrir la fenêtre.   They can open the window.

> **Key Point**
>
> Remember not to pronounce the **x**, **t**, **s** and **z** at the end of the verb.
>
> Also, do not pronounce the **ent** in **ils veulent** or **ils peuvent**.

Devoir (to have to / must)

- **je dois…**   I must…
  tu dois…   you must…
  il / elle / on doit…   he / she / one must…
  nous devons…   we must…
  vous devez…   you must…
  ils / elles doivent…   they must…
- **Je dois faire mes devoirs.**   I must do my homework.
  Elle doit travailler dur.   She must work hard.
  On doit faire attention en classe.   One must pay attention in class.
  Nous devons arriver à l'heure.   We must arrive on time.

> **Key Point**
>
> Don't confuse **devoir** (to have to) with **les devoirs** (homework).

Modal Verbs in the Negative

- **Je ne veux pas aller au collège.**   I don't want to go to school.
  Elle ne peut pas écouter le prof.   She can't hear the teacher.
  On ne doit pas manger en classe.   One must not eat in class.

Some Key Uses of Modal Verbs

- Asking somebody out using **vouloir**:
  Tu veux aller au cinéma?   Do you want to go to the cinema?
  Tu veux jouer au tennis?   Do you want to play tennis?
  Oui, je veux bien.   Yes, I'd love to.
- Asking permission using **pouvoir**:
  Je peux aller aux toilettes?   Can I go to the toilet?
  Je peux te parler?   Can I speak to you?
  Tu peux me prêter un stylo?   Can you lend me a pen?
- Making excuses using **devoir**:
  Je dois faire mes devoirs.   I must do my homework.
  Je dois me laver les cheveux.   I must wash my hair.
  Je ne dois pas être en retard.   I mustn't be late.

> **Quick Test**
>
> 1. Choose the correct form of vouloir below.
>   **Vous voulons / voulez / veulent aller à la cantine?**
> 2. Translate the following into French:
>   I can't do my homework.
> 3. Translate the following into English:
>   **Au collège, on ne doit pas porter de jean.**
> 4. Which is the odd one out and why?
>   a) **Je veux travailler.**
>   b) **Il ne peut pas travailler.**
>   c) **Je dois travailler.**

Faire, Aller and the Immediate Future

You must be able to:

- Form the verbs **aller** and **faire** correctly
- Use **aller** with infinitives of other verbs to talk about the future
- Use other expressions to talk about future plans.

Faire and Aller

- These two verbs are irregular verbs and, together with **avoir** and **être,** are important for you to know.

Faire (to do, make)

- je fais...   I do...
  tu fais...   you do...
  il / elle / on fait...   he / she / one does...
  nous faisons...   we do...
  vous faites...   you do...
  ils / elles font...   they do...
- Je fais mes devoirs.   I'm doing my homework.
  Ils font un gâteau.   They're making a cake.
  Elle fait du vélo.   She's going cycling.

- Note that faire is used in many weather expressions:
  Il fait chaud et il fait beau.   It's hot and it's fine.

Aller (to go)

- je vais...   I go...
  tu vas...   you go...
  il / elle / on va...   he / she / one goes...
  nous allons...   we go...
  vous allez...   you go...
  ils / elles vont...   they go...
- Je vais au cinéma.   I'm going to the cinema.
  Ils vont chez eux.   They're going to their house.
  Elle va à l'école à pied.   She's going to school on foot.

The Immediate Future

- You can use the verb **aller** followed by the infinitive of another verb to talk about what you are going to do in the future.

- **Je vais** *faire du* **shopping.**   I'm going to go shopping.
  Tu vas *jouer au* **foot avec moi?**   Are you going to play football with me?

  Nous allons *voir* **le film.**   We're going to see the film.
  Elles vont *acheter* **des vêtements.**   They're going to buy clothes.

Other Ways of Expressing the Future

- All the following verbs are also followed by the infinitive.
  Je veux   I want
  Je voudrais   I'd like to
  J'espère   I hope to
- **Je veux aller à l'université.**   I want to go to university.
  Je voudrais devenir médecin.   I'd like to become a doctor.
  J'espère travailler en France.   I hope to work in France.
- These expressions are followed by **de** and the infinitive:
  Je rêve de devenir professeur.   I dream of becoming a teacher.
  J'ai l'intention de travailler dur.   I intend to work hard.

Using Faire with Another Verb

- **Faire** can be used with the infinitive of another verb to mean to make someone do something:
  Tu me fais rire.   You make me laugh.
  Le film me fait pleurer.   The film makes me cry.

Quick Test

1. What does this sentence mean in English?
   Ils font les devoirs de maths mais ils ne vont pas finir les devoirs d'anglais.
2. Translate the following into French:
   I'm going to watch television.
3. Which of these is NOT an infinitive:
   a) faire   b) allez   c) manger
4. Which is the odd one out and why?
   a) **Je vais faire du shopping.**
   b) **Je veux faire du shopping.**
   c) **Je fais du shopping.**

Imperative and Reflexive Verbs

You must be able to:

- Tell people what to do correctly
- Recognise reflexives verbs
- Use reflexive verbs correctly, with the correct pronoun.

The Imperative

- This is the form of the verb you use to tell people what to do.
- To do this you need the **tu** or **vous** form of the verb, Use **tu** for one person or **vous** for more than one person or if you want to be polite.
- **tu finis**   you finish

  Take away the **tu** or **vous** and you change it into an order.

Finis tes devoirs!	Finish your homework!
tu sors	you go out
Sors tout de suite!	Get out immediately!
vous mangez	you eat
Mangez plus de légumes!	Eat more vegetables!
vous allez	you go
Allez chez le dentiste!	Go to the dentist's!

- Note that **–er** verbs lose the **–s** of the **tu** form.

tu regardes	you look at
Regarde-moi!	Look at me!

- To tell someone not to do something, put **ne...pas** around the verb.

Ne joue pas au rugby!	Don't play rugby!
Ne sortez pas!	Don't go out.

Key Point

You can also use the nous form of the verb (without the nous) to say let's do something.

Dansons! Let's dance!

Allons au cinéma. Let's go to the cinema.

Regardons le match. Let's watch the match.

Reflexive Verbs

- These are verbs that have **se** in front of them in the infinitive. However, the **se** will change depending on who is doing the action.
- **Se laver** means to wash oneself or to have a wash.

Je me lave.	I'm having a wash.
Tu te laves.	You're having a wash.
Il / elle se lave.	He/she's having a wash.
Nous nous lavons.	We're having a wash.
Vous vous lavez.	You're having a wash.
Ils / elles se lavent.	They're having a wash.

Common Reflexive Verbs

- **se réveiller** — to wake up
- **se lever** — to get up
- **s'appeler** — to be called
- **se doucher** — to have a shower
- **s'habiller** — to get dressed
- **se coucher** — to go to bed
- Note that in front of a vowel **me**, **te** and **se** change to **m'**, **t'** and **s'**.

  Comment t'appelles-tu? — What are you called?

  Elle se lève à sept heures. — She gets up at seven o'clock.

  Ils se couchent à dix heures. — They go to bed at ten o'clock.

- **se laver** — to have a wash
- **se brosser les dents** — to brush your teeth
- **se brosser les cheveux** — to brush your hair
- **se reposer** — to rest
- **se relaxer** — to relax
- **s'arrêter** — to stop
- **se promener** — to go for a walk
- **Nous nous reposons dans le jardin.** — We are resting in the garden.
- **Le bus s'arrête devant la gare.** — The bus stops in front of the station.
- **Tu te relaxes en vacances?** — Do you relax on holiday?
- **Les frères s'appellent Jean et Thomas.** — The brothers are called Jean and Thomas.

Key Point

Reflexive verbs have a special form of the imperative.

Lève-toi!	Get up!
Lave-toi!	Have a wash!
Asseyez-vous!	Sit down!
Réveillez-vous!	Wake up!

Quick Test

1. What does this sentence mean in English?
   Elle se réveille, elle se lève, elle se douche et elle s'habille dans la chambre.
2. Translate the following into French:
   He gets up at six o'clock and he goes to bed at half past nine.
3. Put these verbs into the imperative (**tu** form):
   a) faire   b) écouter   c) manger
4. Put these verbs into the imperative (**vous** form):
   a) aller   b) finir   c) danser

Perfect Tense

You must be able to:
- Form the perfect tense correctly
- Use some irregular past participles
- Know which verbs use être in the perfect tense.

The Perfect Tense with Avoir

- This tense is for talking about something which happened in the past.
- You form the perfect tense by using the present tense of **avoir (j'ai, tu as, il / elle a, nous avons, vous avez, ils / elles ont)** with a special form of the verb called the **past participle**.
- For all **–er** verbs, to form the past participle take off the **–r** and make the **e** into **é**.

manger	to eat
mangé	ate (past participle)
jouer	to play
joué	played (past participle)
danser	to dance
dansé	danced (past participle)

j'ai joué	I have played or I played
tu as joué	you have played or you played
il / elle a joué	he/she has played or he/she played
nous avons joué	we have played or we played
vous avez joué	you have played or you played
ils / elles ont joué	they have played or they played

Key Point

To use a perfect tense in the negative, you make avoir negative: **Je n'ai pas mangé.** I didn't eat.

Ils n'ont pas vu le film. They didn't see the film.

Non –er Verbs

- If the verb does not end in –er, you will have to learn the past participle.
- **Boire** (to drink) becomes **bu:**
  elle a bu de la limonade — she drank lemonade
- **Voir** (to see) becomes **vu:**
  nous avons vu le film — we saw the film
- **Faire** (to do) becomes **fait:**
  ils ont fait un gâteau — they have made a cake
- **Finir** (to finish) becomes **fini:**
  tu as fini? — have you finished?
- **Attendre** (to wait) becomes **attendu:**
  j'ai attendu le bus — I waited for the bus

Verbs with Être

- A small number of verbs take **être** instead of **avoir** in front of the past participle.
- With these verbs, you use the present tense of **être (je suis, tu es, il / elle est, nous sommes, vous êtes, ils / elles sont)** then the past participle.
- The most common of these is the verb **aller**.
- With **être** verbs the past participle agrees as if it was an adjective.

je suis allé	I've gone / I went (masculine)
je suis allée	I've gone / I went (feminine)
tu es allé	you've gone / you went (masculine)
tu es allée	you've gone / you went (feminine)
il est allé	he's gone / he went
elle est allée	she's gone / she went
nous sommes allés	we've gone / we went (masculine)
nous sommes allées	we've gone / we went (feminine)
vous êtes allé	you've gone / you went (masculine polite)
vous êtes allée	you've gone / you went (feminine polite)
vous êtes allés	you've gone / you went (masculine plural)
vous êtes allées	you've gone / you went (feminine plural)
ils sont allés	they've gone / they went (masculine)
elles sont allées	they've gone / they went (feminine)

Key Point

One way of remembering all the verbs which take **être** is MRS VAN DER TRAMP.

monter	to go up
rester	to stay
sortir	to go out
venir	to come
arriver	to arrive
naître	to be born
descendre	to come down
entrer	to enter
retourner	to return
tomber	to fall
rentrer	to go home
aller	to go
mourir	to die
partir	to set off

Common Être Verbs

- **sortir** — to go out
  je suis sorti(e) — I went out
- **arriver** — to arrive
  elle est arrivée — she has arrived
- **partir** — to set off
  ils sont partis — they've left
- **rester** — to stay
  Tu es resté(e) à la maison? — Did you stay at home?

Quick Test

1. Translate this sentence into English.
   Elle a vu le film mais elle n'a pas mangé de popcorn.
2. Translate the following into French:
   I played football, watched TV and finished my homework.
3. Put these verbs into the perfect tense (**je** form):
   a) faire   b) écouter   c) boire
4. Put these verbs into the perfect tense (**elle** form):
   a) aller   b) rester   c) sortir

Review Questions

Shopping and Money

1 List the items of clothing that the boy in the picture is wearing.

[3]

2 Name these materials in English.

a) en coton

b) en cuir

c) en laine [3]

3 Rewrite the following sentence, inserting the adjective '**joli**' into the correct place:

Je porte un chapeau. [1]

4 Name in French three chores that you do at home. [3]

5 Describe two things you spend your money on and describe why. [4]

6 Translate into French.

a) a blue dress

b) a white jumper

c) a green skirt

d) black shoes [4]

Where I Live

1 Find the word to do with shopping in each set of words.

a) A la gare   B le marché   C la banque

b) A le magasin   B le musée   C le théâtre

c) A le centre commercial   B l'église   C l'hôpital

d) A la boulangerie   B le jardin public   C l'aéroport   [4]

2 Complete the following sentences with one of the words marked A, B, or C.

a) Je veux nager…

A au gymnase   B au café   C à la piscine

b) Je vais manger…

A à la banque   B au restaurant   C au musée

c) Je vais acheter un billet de train…

A à la gare   B à l'église   C au cinéma

d) Je veux faire une promenade…

A au parc   B à la piscine   C aux toilettes   [4]

3 Match two halves to complete the sentences.

a) **On doit réduire la pollution et…**   A   **pour aider les piétons.**

b) **Il faut réduire le nombre de voitures…**   B   **plus d'arbres.**

c) **Il faut planter…**   C   **recycler les déchets.**   [3]

Review Questions

Holidays

1 Translate these country names into French using the correct article **le / la / l'**.

a) **France**   b) **Portugal**

c) **Italy**   d) **Scotland**

e) **England**   f) **Spain**

[6]

2 Fill in the gaps with **en / au / aux**.

a) **Normalement je vais en vacances _____ Italie.**

b) **Cette année nous allons _____ France pour deux semaines.**

c) **Ma cousine habite _____ États-Unis.**

d) **D'habitude je passe mes vacances _____ Inde.**

e) **Es-tu déjà allé _____ Afrique?**   [5]

3 Look at the details in the table below and write what each person would say about their holiday.

	Country	Who with	Duration	Transport	Accommodation	Activity
Sophie	Italy	My cousins	Ten days	Train	Hotel	Beach
David	United States	My grandparents	Two weeks	Plane	Hotel	Relaxing
Marcel	France	My parents	Seven days	Car	Campsite	Beach

Sophie: **Je passe mes vacances en Italie avec mes cousins pendant dix jours. Je voyage en train. Je loge dans un hôtel et je vais à la plage.**

David:

Marcel: [10]

4 What are the questions?

a) **Je vais en vacances aux États-Unis.**

b) **J'y vais avec ma famille.**

c) **Je loge chez ma tante.**

d) **Normalement je vais à la plage.**   [4]

Global Issues

1 Complete the table of imperatives:

French	English
Agissez!	Do something / take action!
Conservez!	
	Avoid!
Jetez!	
Protégez!	
	Reduce!
	Respect!
Sauvez!	

[7]

2 When would you use an adverb of quantity and can you give an example of one? [2]

3 Complete these phrases relating to problems or issues.

a) **Il y a trop de** _____

b) **Il n'y a pas de** _____ [2]

4 Complete these sentences:

a) **Ce qui me préoccupe le plus, c'est** _____

b) **Je m'inquiète de** _____ [2]

5 Complete each sentence with the correct infinitive.

protéger	utiliser	recycler	jeter

a) **Il faut** _____ **les transports en commun.**

b) **Il faut** _____ **le verre.**

c) **Il faut** _____ **les animaux.** [3]

Practice Questions

Gender, Plurals and Adjectives

1 Fill in the gaps with **le / la / l'** or **les**.

a) _____ **famille**   b) _____ **chien**

c) _____ **maison**   d) _____ **cuisine**

e) _____ **enfants**   f) _____ **chambre**

g) _____ **jardin**   h) _____ **pièces**

i) _____ **France**   j) _____ **Etats-Unis**   [10]

2 Put the following phrases into the plural form.

a) **une maison blanche** _____

b) **un chien noir** _____

c) **une souris grise** _____

d) **un cheval marron** _____

e) **un chat roux** _____   [5]

3 Write the correct form of the adjectives.

a) **une** _____ **fille (petit)**

b) **Ma sœur est** _____ **(timide).**

c) **Mes frères sont très** _____ **(sportif).**

d) **Mon père a les yeux** _____ **(marron).**

e) **J'habite dans une** _____ **maison (grand).**   [5]

4 Translate the following sentences.

a) I have brown hair.   **J'ai les** _____

b) I live in a white house.   **J'habite dans** _____

c) My sister is tall.   **Ma soeur est** _____

d) I have a little grey mouse.   **J'ai** _____

e) Marc is taller than Léo.   **Marc est** _____ **Léo.**   [5]

Avoir, Être and Common Verbs

1 Fill in the gaps with the correct form of être and avoir.

a) Nous _____ une grande maison.   b) Je _____ très grande.

c) Tu _____ un animal?   d) Vous _____ française?

e) Mes sœurs _____ dix ans.   [5]

2 Complete the sentences with the correct form of the verb in brackets.

a) Tu _____ au foot. (jouer)

b) Mes sœurs _____ Maria et Anna. (s'appeler)

c) Je _____ à cinq heures. (finir)

d) Elle _____ sa mère. (attendre)

e) Vous _____ le français? (aimer)   [5]

3 Complete the sentences using **Il y a, il n'y a pas de,** or **c'est**.

a) _____ une patinoire dans ma ville?

b) J'adore la musique pop _____ fantastique.

c) _____ un restaurant dans l'hôtel?

d) _____ télévision dans ma chambre.

e) _____ cinq personnes dans ma famille.   [5]

4 Translate into French.

a) I am cold. _____   b) My sister is 15. _____

c) Are you thirsty? _____   d) They are very hot. _____

e) How old are they? _____   [5]

5 Translate into French.

a) I watch   b) she waits

c) we like   d) I am playing

e) they are eating   [5]

Practice Questions

Modal Verbs, Faire and Immediate Future

1 Complete the sentences with the correct form of the verb in brackets.

  a) Je _____ faire du shopping. (vouloir)

  b) Tu _____ jouer au foot? (pouvoir)

  c) Elle _____ aller chez ses grands-parents. (devoir)

  d) Elles _____ acheter des cadeaux de Noël. (vouloir)

  e) Nous _____ travailler dur. (devoir)

  f) Vous _____ m'aider? (pouvoir)   [6]

2 Choose the correct form of the verb faire.

  a) Tu fais / fait / faites souvent du vélo?

  b) Il fais / fait / font très chaud aujourd'hui.

  c) Qu'est-ce que vous faisons / faites / font samedi?

  d) Ils fais / fait / font leurs devoirs dans le salon.

  e) Je fais / fait / font une longue promenade à la campagne.   [5]

3 Rewrite these sentences in the immediate future using the correct form of **aller** and the infinitive.

  Eg: **Je mange des frites.**
         Je vais manger des frites.

  a) **Je regarde la télé.**

  b) **Tu écoutes de la musique?**

  c) **Il joue au foot.**

  d) **Nous allons au parc.**

  e) **Est-ce que vous travaillez?**

  f) **Les filles font du shopping.**   [6]

Imperatives, Reflexives, Past Tense

1 Tell these people what to do by choosing the correct imperative from the box.

écoutez	fais	mange	regarde	fermez	ouvrez

a) Il fait froid _____ la porte!

b) Il fait chaud _____ la fenêtre!

c) _____ tes légumes!

d) Va dans ta chambre et _____ tes devoirs!

e) Soyez poli et _____ le professeur!

f) _____ la télé avec moi!   [6]

2 Complete the sentences with the correct pronoun – **me, m', te, t', se s', nous** or **vous**.

a) Je _____ appelle Thomas.

b) Les filles _____ lèvent tard.

c) Tu _____ couches à quelle heure?

d) Il _____ habille très vite.

e) Vous _____ réveillez à quelle heure?   [5]

3 Rewrite these present tense sentences in the past tense.

a) Je mange beaucoup de pommes.

b) Je vais au club des jeunes.

c) Je regarde le match de foot.

d) J'arrive en retard.

e) Je finis mes devoirs.

f) Je fais de la natation.

g) Je sors avec mes amis.

h) Je danse avec Paul.   [8]

Future Tense

You must be able to:

- Tell the difference between the future tense and immediate tense
- Use regular verbs in the future tense
- Use irregular verbs in the future tense.

Future Tense vs Immediate Future

- The future tense is different from the immediate future. The future tense is translated as I will do something. The immediate future is translated as I am going to do something.
- Future tense for regular verbs:
  Firstly, you need the stem, which for regular verbs is the infinitive. Secondly, you need the ending, which changes depending on the subject of the sentence.

Key Point

When forming the future tense using **re** verbs, the last **e** is removed before adding the future ending.

For example: **vendre** becomes **je vendrai**

Subject	Future stem of *jouer*	Ending	Future tense of *jouer*
je	jouer	ai	je jouerai
tu	jouer	as	tu joueras
il / elle / on	jouer	a	il / elle / on jouera
nous	jouer	ons	nous jouerons
vous	jouer	ez	vous jouerez
ils / elles	jouer	ont	ils / elles joueront

Worked Example

To work out how to say 'she will listen' in French:
1. Is the infinitive regular?
   The infinitive is **écouter** (it is a regular verb).
2. What is the subject of the sentence?
   The subject is **elle**.
3. Work out the ending of the verb.
   The ending is **a**.
4. Put it all together.
   Elle écoutera.

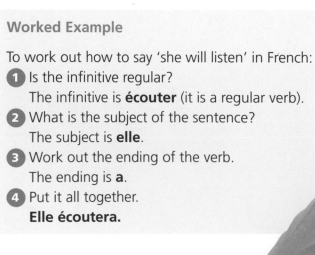

Irregular Verbs

- The stems for irregular verbs need to be learnt individually.
- Here are some common irregular verbs (the same endings are used for regular and irregular verbs):

Irregular Infinitive	Irregular Stem	Example
aller	ir	vous irez
avoir	aur	nous aurons
être	ser	il sera
faire	fer	elle fera
voir	verr	tu verras
venir	viendr	je viendrai

Key Point

Irregular verbs, particularly **être, avoir, aller** and **faire** are extremely important and are used frequently – they must be learnt!

Worked Example

To work out how to say 'we will go' in French:
1. Is the infinitive regular?
   The infinitive is **aller** (an irregular verb) so the stem is **ir**.
2. What is the subject of the sentence?
   The subject is **nous**.
3. Work out the ending.
   The ending is **ons**.
4. Put it all together!
   Nous irons.

Worked Example

To work out how to say 'they will be' in French:
1. Is the infinitive regular?
   The infinitive is **être** (an irregular verb) so the stem is **ser**.
2. What is the subject of the sentence?
   The subject is **ils**.
3. Work out the ending.
   The ending is **ont**.
4. Put it all together!
   Ils seront.

Quick Test

1. What is used as the stem of the future tense?
2. Can you think of three irregular verbs not listed above?
3. What are the six different future tense endings?
4. Translate the following into English: **Nous aurons**.
5. Translate the following into French: She will finish (**finir**).

Pronouns

You must be able to:

- Understand the difference between various types of pronoun
- Pick the correct pronoun to use in a given phrase
- Correctly place the pronoun into the phrase.

What is a Pronoun?

- A pronoun is a word that *replaces* a noun (a naming word).
- There are two types of pronoun – personal and impersonal.
- Pronouns change depending on the noun they are replacing.

Key Point

When using direct and indirect object pronouns, the pronoun comes before the verb and before an auxiliary in the perfect tense.

Personal Pronouns

- A personal pronoun is used instead of a person or a thing.

Subject	Direct Object	Indirect object	Emphatic
je	me	me	moi
tu	te	te	toi
il elle on	le la	lui	lui elle soi
nous	nous	nous	nous
vous	vous	vous	vous
ils elles	les	leur	eux elles

Examples

- *Subject:* The person or thing doing the action
  Elle joue   She plays
  Tu écoutes   You listen
- *Direct object:* Replaces the direct object of the verb
  Je le vois   I see him
  Nous la regardons   We watch it (it refers to the TV, a feminine word)
- *Indirect object:* Replaces an object linked to the verb by **à**
  Je lui parle   I speak to him

- Emphatic: used to emphasize a subject pronoun, as a one word answer to a question or after prepositions.

Moi, je n'aime pas danser.   Me, I don't like dancing.
Qui aime la glace? Moi!   Who likes ice-cream? Me!
Il va chez elle.   He is going to her house.

Impersonal Pronouns

- **y** (there)
  y replaces **à** + a place
  Il va à l'église.   He goes to the church.
  Il y va.   He goes there.
- **en** (some / any)
  en replaces **du / de la / des** + a noun
  Tu veux des frites?   Do you want some chips?
  Oui, j'en voudrais.   Yes I would like some.
- **en** is most often used to replace *things* rather than people or animals.
- Use **de** (of) when talking about people
  Je me souviens de lui   I remember him.
  Je me souviens d'eux.   I remember them.

Reflexive Pronouns

- Reflexive verbs require a pronoun before the verb to indicate that the subject performs this action to him / herself.
- **Je me réveille**   I wake up
- **Il se lève**   He gets up

Subject	Reflexive Pronoun
je	me
tu	te
il / elle / on	se
nous	nous
vous	vous
ils / elles	se

> **Quick Test**
>
> 1. What kind of word does a pronoun substitute?
> 2. Would it matter if the noun was feminine rather than masculine?
> 3. When would it be appropriate to use **lui** in a sentence?
> 4. Which pronoun would you use to substitute a place?

Imperfect Tense

You must be able to:

- Narrate events in the past
- Tell the difference between the perfect tense and imperfect tense
- Use regular and irregular verbs in the imperfect tense.

Imperfect Tense vs Perfect Tense

- Both are past tenses.
- The perfect tense describes a single action in the past.
- The imperfect tense describes:
  - **a)** Something you used to do
  - **b)** A repeated action in the past
  - **c)** A description of the past, e.g. weather and opinions.

> **Key Point**
>
> In speech, it is important to note the pronunciation of the **ais** and **aient** ending on imperfect tense in the **je** and **ils / elles** form. The **'s'** and the **'nt'** are silent letters.

Worked Example

À l'école primaire Luc jouait *(imperfect tense)* **pour une équipe mais un jour il s'est cassé** *(perfect tense)* **la jambe**.

1 The *imperfect tense* is used here because Luc played football over a period of time therefore it was a repeated action.

2 The *perfect tense* is used here because breaking his leg was a single and completed action.

Imperfect Tense

- To form the imperfect tense, two parts are needed:
  The stem: to form this, take the **nous** form of the present tense and remove the **ons** ending.
  The following table shows imperfect stems for some common verbs.
  The ending changes depending on the subject of the sentence.

Verb Group	Infinitive	Stem
er	regarder	regard
ir	choisir	choisiss
re	attendre	attend
irregular	être	et
irregular	avoir	av
irregular	faire	fais
irregular	aller	all

The Imperfect Endings

- je   – ais
  tu   – ais
  il / elle   – ait
  nous   – ions
  vous   – iez
  ils / elles   – aient

Worked Examples

To work out how to say 'he used to watch' in French:

1 What is the **nous** form of the present tense?
The **nous** form of the present tense is **regardons**.

2 Take off the **'ons'**.
The stem is **regard**.

3 What is the subject of the sentence?
The subject is **il**.

4 Work out the ending.
The ending is **ait**.

5 Put it all together.
Il regardait.

To work out how to say 'you used to have' in French:

1 What is the **nous** form of the present tense?
The **nous** form of the present tense is **avons**.

2 Take off the **'ons'**.
The stem is **av**.

3 What is the subject of the sentence?
The subject is **vous**.

4 Work out the ending.
The ending is **iez**.

5 Put it all together.
Vous aviez.

Quick Test

1. What is used as the stem of the imperfect tense?
2. When should you use the imperfect tense?
3. The imperfect tense is used to describe weather in the past: true or false?
4. Can you think of five different imperfect tense endings?
5. Put the following imperfect tense phrase into French: We used to visit.

Conditional Tense and Passive Voice

You must be able to:

- Use the conditional tense
- Form 'si' clauses using the imperfect and the conditional tense
- Use the passive voice in a range of tenses and understand its effect on a sentence.

Conditional Tense

- The conditional tense is used to say what would happen in a specific unknown situation.
- To form the conditional tense:
  The *stem:* use the same stem as for the future tense.
  The *ending:* use the same endings as for the imperfect tense.

> ### Key Point
>
> The future and conditional tense stem for regular verbs is the infinitive.
>
> For irregular verbs, the stem varies, the appropriate stems can be found in the future tense section.

Worked Examples

To work out how to say 'I would hate' in French:

1 What is the stem of the verb?
The stem for regular verbs is the infinitive: **détester**.

2 What is the subject of the sentence?
The subject is **je**.

3 What is the ending in the imperfect tense?
The ending is **ais**.

4 Put it all together.
Je détesterais.

To work out how to say 'I would see' in French:

1 What is the stem of the verb?
The stem for irregular verbs is the same as those for future tense: **verr**.

2 What is the subject of the sentence?
The subject is **je**.

3 What is the ending in the imperfect tense? The ending is **ais**.

4 Put it all together **Je verrais**.

Si Clauses

- **Si** means if.
- The most common **si** clause uses the imperfect and the conditional tense.
- **Si je gagnais à la loterie, j'achèterais une voiture**
  If I won the lottery, I would buy a car.

Passive

- The passive is used when the verb is actioned *on* the subject of the sentence.
- The subject of the sentence is preceded by the preposition **par** (by).
- The *active* voice: James kicks the ball.
- The *passive* voice: The ball is kicked by James.

Forming the Passive

- The passive voice is formed using **être** in the appropriate tense and the past participle.
- Present tense passive voice:

  Le dessin animé est regardé par Lucas. The cartoon is watched by Lucas.

- Past tense passive voice:

  Le dessin animé a été regardé par Lucas. The cartoon was watched by Lucas.

- Future tense passive voice:

  Le dessin animé sera regardé par Lucas. The cartoon will be watched by Lucas.

Preceding Direct Object

- When using the passive voice, the verb must agree with the noun it is acting upon.
- For feminine objects add an extra **e**.
- For masculine plural objects add an **s**.
- For feminine plural objects add an **es**.

Examples

- **Le sac est pris par le voleur.** The bag is taken by the thief.
- **La viande est mangée par Éric.** The meat is eaten by Éric.
- **Les hamburgers seront cuisinés par mon père.** The hamburgers will be cooked by my dad.

> **Quick Test**
>
> 1. What two parts do you need to form the conditional tense?
> 2. What does the following sentence mean?
>   **Si je jouais le match, je gagnerais le concours.**
> 3. Can you change the following sentence from the active voice into the passive voice?
>   Carla ate the sandwich.
> 4. How would you translate the following sentence?
>   **Le film a été vu par Simone.**

Practice Questions

Future Tense and Pronouns

1 Which two parts of a verb do you need to form the future tense?

a)

b) [2]

2 What is the difference between the future tense and the immediate future? Give an example of each. [3]

3 Which pronoun is used to replace a place name? [1]

4 One example of an emphatic pronoun is **moi**, write three more. [3]

5 Rewrite the following sentence, replacing the noun with a direct object pronoun.

Je mange une banane. [1]

6 Put the following phrases into the future tense:

a) I will play .... (**jouer**)

b) She will finish .... (**finir**)

c) We will learn .... (**apprendre**) [3]

Imperfect, Conditional and Passive

1　Would you use the perfect tense or the imperfect tense to translate the following sentence into French? Give a reason for your choice.

I ate cereal for breakfast this morning. [2]

2　When do you use the conditional tense? [2]

3　Complete the following phrases with the correct verb in the imperfect tense.

a) Je _____ **au foot.**

b) Il _____ **à la piscine.**

c) Nous _____ **très sympas.** [3]

4　Change the following phrase from the active voice into the passive voice:

Carla mange du gâteau. [2]

5　Translate the following sentence and label the tenses:

Si j'étais riche, j'achèterais un château. [3]

6　Spot the mistake in the following sentence and rewrite it correctly.

Louise est detesté par Simon. [1]

Gender, Plurals, Adjectives and Adverbs

1 Fill in the gaps with **un, une ou des**?

a) _____ mère   b) _____ fille

c) _____ enfants   d) _____ bateau

e) _____ chiens   f) _____ jardin

g) _____ maison   h) _____ ordinateur

i) _____ tables   j) _____ souris   [10]

2 Choose the correct word to complete the sentences.

a) **Ma sœur est petit / petite.**   b) **J'ai un gros chien blanc / blanche.**

c) **J'ai des poissons rouge / rouges.**   d) **Mon / ma chat s'appelle Fluffy.**

e) **Mon / mes parents sont gentils.**   f) **J'ai les cheveux marron / brun.**   [6]

3 Join two halves to make correct sentences.

a)	**J' ai une souris**		**petit chien blanc**
b)	**Nous avons un gros**		**tortue**
c)	**Ma sœur a une**		**grise**
d)	**Je n'aime pas les grosses**		**chien noir**
e)	**J' ai un**		**souris**

[5]

4 Complete the sentences.

a) **J'ai** _____ (a brown cat)   b) **J'habite dans** _____ (a little house)

c) **Ma sœur a** _____ (brown eyes)   d) **Ma chambre est** _____ (big and blue)

e) **Mes chats sont** _____ (small and white)   [5]

5 Here are some details about Anna. Write out what Anna would say about herself.

> Blue eyes, tall, two sisters, a big white house, two brown dogs and two little grey mice

Bonjour je m'appelle Anna.

J'ai _____ **et je suis** _____ **J'ai** _____

J'habite dans _____ **J'ai** _____ **et** _____   [6]

Avoir, Être and Common Verbs

1 Fill in the gaps with appropriate form of **avoir**.

a) Nous .... un chat.

b) Mes sœurs .... les cheveux blonds.

c) Tu .... un frère?

d) J' .... les yeux bleus.

e) Mon père .... une voiture rouge. [5]

2 Fill in the gaps with the appropriate form of **être**.

a) Ma sœur .... sympa.

b) Je .... très grande.

c) Dans ma chambre, mon lit .... entre mon armoire et mon bureau.

d) Où .... mes chaussures?

e) Les cheveux de ma mère .... noirs. [5]

3 Match the two halves.

a)	Nous	aimes le chocolat?
b)	Vous	regardent souvent la télé.
c)	Tu	attendez qui?
d)	Elle	finissons tous les jours à 15.30.
e)	Mes sœurs	travaille bien à l'école.

[5]

4 Translate into French.

a) My mum is 45.   b) My sisters are 10 and 13.   c) I am hungry.

d) Are you thirsty?   e) We are cold. [5]

5 Translate the verbs into English.

a) Je joue au foot tous les jours après l'école.

b) Qu'est-ce que tu fais? Je révise pour mon test demain.

c) Normalement je voyage en train mais cette année on voyage en avion.

d) J'écoute de la musique. [6]

Review Questions

Modal Verbs, Faire, Immediate Future

1 Fill in the space with the correct form of the modal verb in brackets.

a) Je _____ voir ce film. (vouloir)

b) Ils ne _____ pas sortir ce soir. (pouvoir)

c) Nous ne _____ pas parler en classe. (devoir)

d) Marie _____ faire du shopping. (vouloir)

e) On _____ prendre le train. (pouvoir)

f) Tu _____ m'écouter! (devoir)   [6]

2 Choose the correct phrase to complete the question.

a) J'adore les magasins parce que j'aime _____

    A faire du vélo.   B faire du shopping.   C faire des promenades.

b) J'adore l'été parce qu'il _____

    A fait froid.   B fait chaud.   C fait mauvais.

c) J'aime aller au bord de la mer pour _____

    A faire de l'alpinisme.   B faire du judo.   C faire de la natation.

                                                                       [3]

3 Choose a sentence from the box to go with each of the sentences below.

| Je vais regarder un film. | Je vais nager. | Je vais aller à la pêche. | Je vais danser. |

a) Je vais à la piscine. _____

b) Je vais à la discothèque. _____

c) Je vais au cinéma. _____

d) Je vais au lac. _____   [4]

Imperatives, Reflexives, Perfect Tense

1 Find the imperative form of the verb in each set of verbs.

a) A manger   B mangé   C mangez

b) A bois   B boire   C bu

c) A fini   B finissent   C finissez

d) A sors   B sort   C sortir

e) A regardé   B regarde   C regarder   [5]

2 Complete the following.

a) **Je me réveille** ....

     A à sept heures.   B dans la salle de bains.   C jamais.

b) **Je me douche** ....

     A dans la cuisine.   B dans la salle de bains.   C dans le jardin.

c) **Nous nous lavons** ....

     A dans le jardin.   B la maison.   C les mains.

d) **A quelle heure** ....

     A je m'appelle?   B il se trouve.   C tu te couches?   [4]

3 Put the following verbs in brackets into the perfect tense. Make any necessary agreements.

a) **J'ai (manger) une banane.**

b) **Nous avons (parler) à son frère.**

c) **Ils ont (boire) du café.**

d) **Elle est (arriver) en retard.**

e) **Les deux filles sont (aller) au centre commercial.**

f) **Est-ce que tu as (finir) tes devoirs?**

g) **Les garçons sont (sortir) avec leurs amis.**

h) **Vous avez (voir) le film?**   [8]

Review Questions

Future Tense and Pronouns

1 The infinitive is used for the stem of all future tense verbs, true or false? [1]

2 When would you use an emphatic pronoun? [1]

3 Which pronoun would you use to replace **du / de la / des** + a noun? [1]

4 Rewrite the following sentence, replacing the noun with a pronoun.

Elle aide ses enfants. [1]

5 Complete the table:

Infinitive	Stem	Future tense phrase
regarder	regarder	il regardera
manger		je
finir		tu
vendre		ils
faire		nous
avoir		elle
aller		vous

[12]

6 Identify each type of pronoun in italics.

a) *Elle* mange une pomme.

b) *Moi*, j'adore les pommes.

c) Elle *la* mange. [3]

Imperfect, Conditional and Passive

1 When would you use the imperfect tense? [2]

2 Complete the table for the imperfect tense:

Subject	Ending	Conjugation of *Visiter*
Je	ais	Je visitais
Tu		
		Il visitait
	ions	
	iez	
Elles		

[10]

3 Which of these sentences is an example of conditional tense?

a) **Elle jouait du piano.**

b) **Ils finiront leurs devoirs.**

c) **Nous écouterions la radio.** [1]

4 Spot the errors in the following conditional tense phrases and rewrite them correctly:

a) **Il mangerais de la pizza.**

b) **Vous perdrions la compétition.** [2]

5 a) Translate the following passive voice sentence:

Le livre est lu par Élodie.

b) And now put it into the active voice. [2]

Mixed Test-Style Questions

1 Reorder the conversation so that it makes sense. Write the letters in order. a) is your starting point.

a) **Salut. Ça va?**

b) **Comme toi, j'ai presque 14 ans car mon anniversaire c'est le 18 mars. Tu habites où?**

c) **J'habite à Londres dans une grande maison. Et toi?**

d) **Oui, parce que c'est très grand.**

e) **J'habite à Leeds, dans le nord de l'Angleterre. Tu aimes Londres?**

f) **Oui ça va merci.**

g) **Je m'appelle Paul. Tu as quel âge?**

h) **Comment t'appelles-tu?**

i) **Je m'appelle Félix et toi? J'ai 13 ans, presque 14 ans. Mon anniversaire c'est le 12 mars.**

j) **Et toi, tu as quel âge?**

8 marks

2 Read what the three people say about themselves, then answer the questions below.

> **Salut! Je m'appelle Christelle et j'habite dans le sud de la France avec ma mère car mes parents sont divorcés. J'ai deux demi-frères qui sont plus âgés que moi. Mon père habite dans le nord de la France. Normalement je vais chez mon père pendant les vacances. J'adore les animaux et je fais de l'équitation deux fois par semaine. C'est chouette. Et toi, tu aimes les animaux?**

> **Salut! Je m'appelle Marco et j'habite en Italie mais je suis né en Angleterre. J'habite avec mes parents mais mon père travaille en Angleterre alors il voyage beaucoup. Je suis fils unique mais je voudrais une sœur. J'adore la musique et je joue du piano et je voudrais apprendre la guitare. Et toi, tu aimes la guitare?**

> **Bonjour! Je m'appelle Lena et j'habite en Espagne. J'ai treize ans et mon anniversaire c'est le 20 mars. J'ai une sœur qui a 10 ans. Elle est très gentille. J'adore la musique pop mais je déteste le rap. Je joue de la guitare. Et toi, tu aimes la musique?**

a) Who has a sister? _____

b) Who doesn't live with their dad? _____

c) Who loves horses? _____

d) Who plays the guitar? _____

e) Who has a younger sister? _____

5 marks

3 Fill in the gaps with the words from the box.

trois	dix	partage	une télévision	génial

Chez moi j'ai (a) _____ pièces. Nous avons (b) _____

chambres. Je (c) _____ ma chambre avec ma sœur. Dans ma chambre,

j'ai (d) _____ et un ordinateur. C'est (e) _____

5 marks

4 Read the conversation and answer the questions in English.

Salut! Tu veux aller à la patinoire mardi?

Oui, à quelle heure?

On y va à la séance de quinze heures?

Ok. Rendez-vous devant le centre sportif à quatorze heures?

Super. À plus….!

a) Where are they going? _____

b) When are they going? _____

c) Where exactly are they meeting up? _____

d) At what time? _____

5 marks

TOTAL

23

Mixed Test-Style Questions

5 Read the text and decide if the sentences are True or False?

Bonjour je m'appelle Ben et je suis né le 10 avril. J'ai quatorze ans. J'ai un frère et une sœur. Ma sœur a douze ans et mon frère a dix-sept ans. J'habite avec mes parents dans une grande maison dans le nord de l'Angleterre. J'aime habiter dans ma maison parce qu'elle est grande et parce que je ne partage pas ma chambre mais je n'aime pas habiter dans le nord de l'Angleterre car il fait froid. Pendant mon temps libre j'aime aller au cinéma avec mes amis. Je joue de la trompette aussi et mon frère joue du piano.

a) Ben was born in winter.   T / F   ☐

b) Ben is the youngest in the family.   T / F   ☐

c) There are 6 people in Ben's family.   T / F   ☐

d) Ben likes his house.   T / F   ☐

e) Ben has his own bedroom.   T / F   ☐

f) Ben plays the piano and the trumpet.   T / F   ☐   ☐

6 marks

6 Match up the two halves of the items below. The first one has been done for you.

For example: **a) une glace à la fraise**

a)	une glace à la		poisson
b)	un thé		lait
c)	un gâteau		fraise
d)	un sandwich		chocolat
e)	une tarte aux		au citron
f)	un café au		abricots
g)	une mousse au		au jambon
h)	la soupe de		au café

☐

7 marks

7 Read what these people say about food and drink, then answer the questions below.

> **Chantal:**
> Je déteste le poisson et les fruits de mer. Je mange rarement du fromage et des pizzas. J'aime bien les haricots, le chou-fleur et les petits pois. Je bois tous les jours du chocolat chaud au petit-déjeuner.

> **Salma:**
> J'aime les pâtes et les pizzas. Je n'aime pas les œufs parce que le goût est affreux. J'aime boire de l'eau minérale parce que c'est bon pour la santé.

> **Oscar:**
> J'adore le steak-frites, c'est mon plat préféré. J'aime aussi manger du poisson.Cependant, je n'aime pas beaucoup les desserts. Je préfère le fromage. Je bois beaucoup de café.

a) Who prefers a cold drink? _____

b) Who likes vegetables? _____

c) Who does not like eating sweet things? _____

d) Who likes Italian food? _____

e) Who would not eat an omelette? _____

f) Who does not like fish? _____

g) Who likes cheese? _____

7 marks

TOTAL

20

Mixed Test-Style Questions

8 Read these definitions and decide what school subject is being talked about.

a) **On apprend les dates.** _____

b) **On étudie les autres pays du monde.** _____

c) **On joue des instruments et on chante des chansons.** _____

d) **On étudie des plantes et des animaux.** _____

e) **On travaille avec des ordinateurs.** _____

f) **On apprend la grammaire de la langue parlée en France.** _____

g) **On joue au foot ou au hockey.** _____

7 marks

9 Read these sentences and say if the statements are positive or negative.

a) **J'ai beaucoup de copains et de copines au collège.** _____

b) **Les professeurs sont ennuyeux.** _____

c) **L'uniforme n'est pas très joli.** _____

d) **Il n'y a pas assez d'ordinateurs.** _____

e) **Je fais beaucoup de progrès.** _____

f) **Les bâtiments sont très vieux et tristes.** _____

g) **Il y a une nouvelle piscine.** _____

h) **Je ne comprends pas mon prof de maths.** _____

8 marks

10 Answer the following questions in French.

a) **Comment s'appelle ton collège?** _____

b) **Où se trouve ton collège?** _____

c) **Combien d'élèves y a-t-il?** _____

d) **À quelle heure commencent les cours?** _____

e) **Qu'est-ce que tu fais pendant la pause-déjeuner?** _____

f) **Comment est ton uniforme?** _____

g) Quelle est ta matière préférée? ....

h) À quelle heure finissent les cours? ....

11 Olivier is talking about sport. Put the five sports he mentions in order according to his preference.

Je n'aime pas tellement le football parce que je le trouve un peu ennuyeux.

Je me passionne pour le rugby, c'est mon sport préféré. Je joue au rugby presque tous les jours.

J'aime aussi le tennis et je joue avec ma sœur deux ou trois fois par semaine.

J'ai horreur du golf. Pour moi, c'est un sport idiot.

J'aime bien la natation, mais je préfère le tennis.

....

....

5 marks

12 Match up the two halves of the sentences below.

a)	Je ne veux pas manger;	j'ai mal aux pieds.
b)	Je ne peux pas faire une promenade;	j'ai mal aux dents.
c)	Je veux une aspirine;	j'ai mal à la gorge.
d)	Je vais chez le dentiste;	j'ai mal à la tête.
e)	Je ne peux pas faire mes devoirs;	j'ai mal à l'estomac.
f)	Je ne peux pas parler;	j'ai mal à la main.

6 marks

TOTAL

34

Mixed Test-Style Questions

13 Correct the following sentences by changing the word in italics.

a) Les fruits et les légumes sont *mauvais* pour la santé.

b) Au petit-déjeuner, je bois du *coca* chaud.

c) Mon *fruit* préféré, c'est le chou.

d) Il faut *manger* beaucoup d'eau.

e) Il ne faut pas *boire* de cigarettes.

5 marks

14 Rearrange the following words to create a sentence about jobs.

pilote	je	parce	c'est	travaille
comme	que	passionnant	très	

5 marks

15 Read what Louis says below and answer the questions in English.

Je m'appelle Louis et en ce moment je travaille comme infirmier mais je voudrais être footballeur car je pense que ce serait bien payé et stimulant.

a) What job does Louis do? ....

b) What would he like to do and why? ....

2 marks

16 Complete the following paragraph with the words from the box.

va	au collège	être	les sciences	examens

En ce moment il va .... et en juin il va passer ses

.... Il .... aller au lycée pour étudier

.... car il veut .... médecin.

5 marks

17 Put these phrases into a logical order by numbering them from 1-5, with 1 being what you would do first:

a) Je vais aller au lycée.

b) Je vais passer mes examens du GCSE.

c) Je vais chercher un emploi.

d) Je vais aller à l'université.

e) Je vais quitter le collège.

5 marks

18 What day and at what time are they meeting up?

a) Rendez-vous mardi à une heure vingt-cinq? ....

b) Rendez-vous mercredi à treize heures quinze? ....

c) On va à la piscine dimanche à midi? ....

d) Viens chez moi lundi à trois heures et demie! ....

e) On y va jeudi à six heures moins le quart? ....

5 marks

19 Read the weather forecast and decide what each person needs to take with them from the images below.

Aujourd'hui…

à Londres il fait beau et il y a du soleil;

à Paris il pleut beaucoup mais il ne fait pas froid;

à Marseille il fait très très chaud! Super pour la plage!

à Sydney, il fait très froid et attention à la neige!

a) I am going to Paris; I need to take ....   b) I live in Sydney; I need to wear a ....

c) I live in Marseille; I need to wear a ....   d) I am going to London today;
                                                               I must remember to take my ....

A   B   C   D

4 marks

TOTAL

31

20 Read the email to a hotel and answer the questions.

Madame, Monsieur,

Je voudrais réserver deux chambres dans votre hôtel du dix-huit juillet au vingt juillet pour deux adultes et trois enfants. Nous aimerions une chambre avec deux lits simples et une chambre avec un lit double et un lit simple. J'ai vu sur le site Internet que le petit-déjeuner est compris dans le prix des chambres. Pouvez-vous confirmer s'il vous plaît? C'est trente-quatre euros par adulte par nuit et vingt-deux euros par enfant par nuit, c'est ça?

Merci
Mme Durand

a) How many rooms is the lady booking? ....

b) How many people in total? ....

c) How many nights are they staying for? ....

d) What has she read about the breakfast? ....

e) The prices are correct. How much would she have to pay for the duration of her stay? ....

☐ 5 marks

21 In French, write two disadvantages of watching TV.

....

....

☐ 4 marks

22 In French, list three things you can do online.

....

....

....

☐ 6 marks

23 Translate the following phrases into French, using the future tense of the verb in brackets.

a) He will listen (**écouter**) ....

b) They (girls) will choose (**choisir**) ....

c) We will lose (**perdre**) ....

☐ 3 marks

24 Read and answer the questions below in English.

Je m'appelle Marine et je crois que l'environnement est vraiment important. En ce moment je trouve que la priorité c'est le réchauffement de la planète et le changement climatique. À mon avis tout le monde doit faire quelque chose, par exemple on doit trier les déchets pour le recyclage et utiliser les transports en commun.

a) What does Marine think the priorities for the environment are?

b) Who does she think should do something?

c) What should be done?

d) Pick out three infinitives from the text and write them in English

8 marks

25 What kind of verb must be used with **il faut**?

1 mark

26 Write the French for each of these adverbs of quantity.

a) enough

b) more

c) too much

d) lots

4 marks

TOTAL

31

Mixed Test-Style Questions

27 Rewrite the sentence below adding a frequency word, a connective, an intensifier and an opinion.

J'aime regarder un dessin animé.

....

....

4 marks

28 Identify the following places in the town.

a) **On peut y changer de l'argent.** ....

b) **On peut y prendre le train.** ....

c) **On peut y emprunter des livres et lire des journaux.** ....

d) **On peut y faire du shopping.** ....

4 marks

29 Match up the two halves of the sentences below.

a)	**Ma ville est animée et**		**pollué.**
b)	**Ma ville est très calme**		**et de restaurants.**
c)	**L'air est sale et**		**et tranquille.**
d)	**Le marché est excellent**		**il y a beaucoup à faire.**
e)	**Il y a beaucoup de cafés**		**si on veut acheter des fruits.**
f)	**Il y a trop de**		**joli.**
g)	**Le jardin public est**		**magasins.**
h)	**Il n'y a pas assez de**		**voitures au centre-ville.**

8 marks

30 Complete the following sentences with an appropriate phrase.

Example: **Je n'aime pas habiter ici parce que…c'est ennuyeux.**

a) **Pour les touristes, il y a…** _____

b) **J'aime habiter ici parce que…** _____

c) **Le soir, comme distractions, il y a…** _____

d) **Pour ceux qui aiment le sport, il y a…** _____

e) **Pour ceux qui aiment faire du shopping, il y a…** _____

5 marks

31 Put the following sentences about daily routine in the correct order.

a) **Je me couche à dix heures.**

b) **Je m'habille et je prends le petit-déjeuner.**

c) **Je me lève et je me douche dans la salle de bains.**

d) **Je me réveille à six heures et demie.**

e) **Après l'école, je me relaxe à la maison puis je fais mes devoirs.**

5 marks

32 Write out these present tense sentences in the perfect tense.

Example: **Je mange une glace.** (present tense)

       J'ai mangé une glace. (perfect tense)

a) **Je regarde la télé.** _____

b) **Tu bois de la limonade.** _____

c) **Il écoute la radio.** _____

d) **Nous travaillons dans le jardin.** _____

e) **Elle finit ses devoirs.** _____

f) **Les deux garçons voient le film.** _____

8 marks

g) **Vous faites du ski?** _____

TOTAL

h) **Je danse avec mes copines.** _____

34

Pronunciation Guide

La Prononciation Française

Knowing key sounds will help you improve your speaking and listening skills. Here is a summary of key French sounds.

Letters	Sounds like.......	Examples
final consonants t / d / b / p / x / s / r / c	silent except **un fils**	**c'est / ans / blanc / les yeux / grand beaucoup / trop**
h	silent	**l'hôtel / l'histoire / heureux**
in / im / un / ain	nasal sound	**un / du pain / un copain important / intelligent / un lapin**
en / em / an / am	nasal sound	**ans / un enfant / dans**
on / om	nasal sound	**bon / une maison / un avion**
qu	k	**quatre / quand / qui**
a	ah	**la table / confortable / âge**
y / i	ee	**un site / une bicyclette**
o / eau / au	oh	**le bateau / le chapeau / les chevaux**
ou	oo	**tout / sous / beaucoup**
oi	wa	**coiffer / le coiffeur / moi**
eu	euh	**les yeux / les cheveux / bleus**
ai / é / er	ay	**une maison / chanter / préféré**

Answers

Page 5 Quick Test
1. Je m'appelle…………et j'ai ………………ans.
2. Comment t'appelles-tu? Quel âge as-tu?
3. beau-père
4. Hello! My name is Anne and I am nearly 13. My birthday is on October 30th. I live in Lille with my parents and my two brothers. My brothers are called Bruno and Pierre and they are 10 and 7 years old.

Page 7 Quick Test
1. J'ai les yeux marron et les cheveux longs.
2. Ma sœur est grande.
3. Je n'ai pas d'animaux.
4. Ma sœur a deux chevaux.

Page 9 Quick Test
1. J'habite dans une maison dans une ville dans le sud de l'Angleterre.
2. Kitchen–feminine; bedroom–feminine; garage–masculine
3. loin
4. Je partage ma chambre avec mon frère.

Page 11 Quick Test
1. un bureau, un lit, un canapé, un ordinateur
2. None. They are all masculine.
3. Mon lit est à côté de mon bureau.
4. J'aide ma mère tous les jours.

Page 13 Quick Test
1. c) un chou (masculine)
2. Je mange tous les jours des pommes.
3. I don't like cabbage because the taste is horrible.
4. c) Les petits pois sont bleus.

Page 15 Quick Test
1. c) des fruits de mer
2. Comme dessert, je prends une glace au chocolat.

> In French when you want to say 'I'll have…+ menu choice' use the verb **prendre** (to take). **Je prends une glace au chocolat** means literally 'I take a chocolate ice cream.'

3. Put a bit of salt on the chips.
4. a) J'ai choisi le steak parce que je suis végétarien.

Page 17 Quick Test
1. d) à la piscine
2. Je me passionne pour le football mais je ne peux pas supporter le rugby.
3. I often go cycling but I never play cards.
4. c) le patinage.

Page 19 Quick Test
1. c) gorge
2. Je suis malade. J'ai mal à la gorge et à la tête.
3. I don't eat too much cheese, it's bad for you.
4. c) je vais fumer des cigarettes.

1. a) violet [1]
   b) vert [1]
   c) gris [1]
   d) rose [1]
2. un, deux, trois, quatre, cinq, six, sept, huit, neuf, dix, onze, douze, treize, quatorze, quinze, seize, dix-sept, dix-huit, dix-neuf, vingt [20]
3. lundi, mardi, mercredi, jeudi, vendredi, samedi, dimanche [7]
4. a) février [1]
   b) avril [1]
   c) juin [1]
   d) août [1]
   e) octobre [1]
   f) décembre [1]
5. a) deux [1]
   b) huit [1]
   c) treize [1]
   d) dix-sept [1]
   e) dix [1]
   f) dix-huit [1]
   g) quatorze [1]
   h) onze [1]
   i) huit [1]
   j) un [1]
6. a) trente 30 [1]
   b) cinquante-et-un 51 [1]
   c) soixante-trois 63 [1]
   d) quatre-vingts 80 [1]
   e) quatre-vingt-dix 90 [1]
7. a) trente-cinq [1]
   b) soixante-six [1]
   c) soixante-quinze [1]
   d) quatre-vingt–quatre [1]
   e) quatre-vingt-dix-neuf [1]
8. a) Il est sept heures [1]
   b) Il est sept heures dix [1]
   c) Il est onze heures et quart [1]
   d) Il est neuf heures et demie [1]
   e) Il est trois heures moins le quart [1]
   f) Il est quatre heures moins cinq [1]
9. a) Il est deux heures [1]
   b) Il est quatre heures dix [1]
   c) Il est cinq heures et quart [1]
   d) Il est dix heures et demie [1]
   e) Il est six heures moins le quart [1]
   f) Il est dix heures moins dix [1]
10. a) C'est quand ton anniversaire? [1]
    b) Deux + deux ça fait combien? [1]
    c) Qui est né en décembre? [1]
    d) Où fait-il chaud en hiver? [1]
    e) Comment dit-on 'janvier' en anglais? [1]
    f) Quelle est la date aujourd'hui? [1]
11. a) Il fait très chaud. [1]
    b) Il y a du soleil. [1]
    c) Il y a du vent. [1]
    d) Il pleut. [1]
    e) Il fait 20 degrés. [1]
    f) Il fait mauvais. [1]
    g) Il y a du brouillard. [1]

Page 22
1. a) Comment t'appelles-tu? Je m'appelle Anna. [1]
   b) Quel âge as-tu? J'ai treize ans. [1]
   c) Tu as des frères et des sœurs? Non, je suis fille unique. [1]

d) Tu as un animal? Oui, j'ai un chien. [1]

e) Comment s'appelle ta mère? Elle s'appelle Maria. [1]

2. **a)** ans [1]

   b) une, frères [2]

   c) bleus, longs [2]

   d) amusants [1]

   e) chien, il [2]

3. Je m'appelle Alexandre. Mon anniversaire c'est le 13.5. (or je suis né le 13.5.) J'habite à Paris. J'ai un frère. J'ai les yeux verts et les cheveux courts et bruns / marron. Je n'ai pas d'animaux [7]

   Je m'appelle Karima. Mon anniversaire c'est le 05.7. (or je suis née le 05.7.2001). J'habite à Marseille. Je n'ai pas de frères ou de sœurs. J'ai les yeux marron et les cheveux longs et noirs. J'ai un chien et il a 2 ans. [7]

Page 23

1. **a)** la cuisine [1]

   b) le salon [1]

   c) la chambre [1]

   d) le grenier [1]

   e) la salle de bains [1]

   f) une chaise [1]

   g) un lit [1]

   h) une armoire [1]

   i) un ordinateur [1]

   j) un bureau [1]

2. **a)** Dans ma chambre il y a un ordinateur. [1]

   b) La télé est sur mon bureau. [1]

   c) Je partage ma chambre avec ma sœur. [1]

   d) Il y a deux canapés dans le salon. [1]

3. J' habite **dans** un grand **appartement** dans une petite **ville** dans le **sud** de l'Angleterre. **J'adore** ma ville. Chez moi, il y a **dix** pièces mais je n'ai pas de **jardin**. Dans ma **chambre** j'ai un **ordinateur** C'est génial. Dans la chambre de ma sœur **il y a** une console. [10]

Page 24

1. apples, chicken, ice-cream [3]

> You don't have to understand every word to get full marks for this task. Read the question carefully and then look for the words that answer the question, i.e. three things that Clémentine does eat, and don't worry about understanding what she does not like to eat.

2. Entrées: Soupe à l'oignon. Plats principaux: Omelette aux champignons: Desserts: Salade de fruits, Boissons: Thé au citron [4]

Page 25

1. **a)** B [1]

   b) C [1]

   c) A [1]

   d) G [1]

   e) E [1]

2. **a)** le tennis [1]

   b) le cyclisme [1]

   c) le rugby [1]

   d) l'équitation [1]

   e) le patinage [1]

3. **a)** mauvais [1]

   b) bon [1]

   c) mauvais [1]

   d) mauvais [1]

   e) bon [1]

   f) mauvais [1]

   g) bon [1]

   h) bon [1]

Page 27 Quick Test

1. **c)** la musique (feminine)

2. J'aime la géographie parce que c'est amusant.

3. I don't like maths because the teacher is bad.

4. **a)** J'aime le dessin, c'est nul.

Page 29 Quick Test

1. **c)** il est interdit

2. On doit mettre une cravate bleue.

3. Lessons finish at half past three.

4. **a)** J'aime l'uniforme, c'est horrible.

Page 31 Quick Test

1. acteur / actrice
   avocat(e)
   chanteur / chanteuse
   coiffeur / coiffeuse
   développeur / développeuse multimédia
   directeur / directrice de magasin
   infirmier / infirmière
   traducteur / traductrice

2. dans un hôpital

3. any person that may work in an office

4. You must / it is necessary to share.

Page 33 Quick Test

1. Je suis fort(e) en
   Je suis intéressé(e) par
   Je m'intéresse à
   J'ai une passion pour
   Je suis accro à

2. health and money

3. I am going to study maths.

4. any answer from the ambitions section in this chapter.

Page 35 Quick Test

1. de la, du

2. Je préfère… / Ma musique préférée c'est…

3. J'aime écouter de la musique classique parce que c'est relaxant.

4. C'est trop lent

Page 37 Quick Test

1. M / F / M / F

2. au centre commercial- à la bibliothèque- au restaurant

3. Tu veux aller à la piscine aujourd'hui à dix heures et demie?

4. Allons au cinéma!

Page 39 Quick Test

1. No more / no longer

2. A frequency word describes how often something occurs (e.g. de temps en temps, le weekend, rarement, souvent, tous les jours, une / deux fois par semaine).

3. I like watching soaps because they are moving.

4. Any frequency word or opinion can be used. e.g. Je regarde un dessin animé tous les jours car c'est marrant.

Page 41 Quick Test

1. J'envoie des SMS. Je téléphone à mes amis. Je joue à desjeux. Je fais des recherches en ligne.

2. You / one / we can.

3. Ça rend accro. On devient mollasson. Il y a trop de violence. Il y a trop de gros mots. On n'a pas assez d'air frais.

4. Ça m'aide à communiquer avec mes amis. C'est plus facile de changer des projets. On peut communiquer plus facilement. On peut se tenir au courant. Je me sens plus en sécurité.

Page 42

1.
   a) ma mère [1]
   b) ma tante [1]
   c) ma grand-mère [1]
   d) mon grand-père [1]
   e) ma sœur [1]

2.
   a) J'ai les cheveux blonds. I have blond hair. [2]
   b) Je suis grande et mince. I am tall and slim. [2]
   c) J'ai quatorze ans. I am fourteen. [2]
   d) J'ai les yeux verts. I have green eyes. [2]

3.
   a) Comment t'appelles-tu? Tu t'appelles comment? Comment tu t'appelles? [1]
   b) Quel âge as-tu? Tu as quel âge? [1]
   c) Quelle est la date de ton anniversaire? C'est quoi la date de ton anniversaire? [1]
   d) Tu as des frères ou des sœurs? As-tu des frères ou des sœurs? [1]
   e) Où habites-tu? Tu habites où? [1]
   f) Tu as un animal? As-tu un animal? [1]

4. **J'ai** douze ans mais ma sœur **a** trois ans. J'ai les **cheveux** longs et les **yeux** marron. Je n'ai pas de **frères**. Mon chien **s'appelle** Polo. [6]

5.
   a) J'ai treize ans. [1]
   b) Mon anniversaire c'est le 15 / quinze juillet. [1]
   c) J'ai les cheveux longs et bruns et les yeux verts. [1]
   d) J'ai un chat blanc. [1]
   e) Mon chat s'appelle Fluffy. [1]

Page 43

1.
   a) à [1]
   b) dans [1]
   c) en [1]
   d) au [1]
   e) dans [1]

2.
   a) J'habite dans une petite maison. [1]
   b) Il y a cinq pièces dans mon appartement. [1]
   c) Je n'ai pas d'ordinateur dans ma chambre. [1]
   d) La télé est sur la table. [1]
   e) La chambre de ma sœur est petite. [1]

3.
   a) Je n'ai pas d'ordinateur dans ma chambre. [1]
   b) Ma chambre n'est pas grande. [1]
   c) Nous n'avons pas de jardin. [1]
   d) Je ne fais pas souvent la vaisselle [1]
   e) Ma sœur n'a pas de console dans sa chambre. [1]

> Remember that when you use **ne...pas de** the **de** always stays the same regardless of whether the word that follows is masculine, feminine or plural.

4.
   a) J'habite dans une grande maison dans le nord de l'Angleterre. [4]
   b) Chez moi / à la maison nous avons dix pièces. [3]
   c) Je range souvent le salon. [3]
   d) Je fais la vaisselle tous les jours mais c'est tres ennuyeux. [4]

Page 44

1.
   a) une fraise [1]
   b) un citron [1]
   c) une pêche [1]
   d) une poire [1]
   e) une pomme [1]

2.
   a) de tomates [1]
   b) une glace [1]
   c) un jus d'orange [1]
   d) les toilettes [1]

3.
   a) légumes [1]
   b) fruits [1]
   c) desserts [1]
   d) viande [1]
   e) viande [1]
   f) fruits [1]
   g) desserts [1]
   h) légumes [1]

Page 45

1. vélo, basketball, natation, hockey, tennis [5]

2.
   a) C'est mauvais pour la santé. [1]
   b) Je veux rester en forme. [1]
   c) J'ai mal aux dents. [1]

3.
   a) Il faut manger de la salade. [1]
   b) Il faut boire de l'eau. [1]
   c) Il ne faut pas manger de biscuits. [1]
   d) Il ne faut pas boire beaucoup de café. [1]
   e) Il faut faire du sport. [1]

Page 46

1.
   a) D [1]
   b) B [1]
   c) A [1]
   d) C [1]

2.
   a) C [1]
   b) B [1]
   c) C [1]
   d) A [1]

Page 47

1.
   a) médecin [1]
   b) professeur [1]
   c) facteur [1]
   d) coiffeur / coiffeuse [1]

2.

Masculine	Feminine
acteur	actrice
avocat	avocate
chanteur	chanteuse
coiffeur	coiffeuse
directeur de magasin	directrice de magasin
infirmier	infirmière
traducteur	traductrice

[7]

3.
   a) poli [1]
   b) stimulant [1]
   c) riche [1]

4. Students' own answers
   2 marks per answer, one for correct verb and one for suitable noun or infinitive [6]

Page 48

1.
   a) du [1]
   b) de la [1]
   c) de la [1]
   d) du [1]
   e) de la [1]

2.   **a)**   Tu veux aller au restaurant? Do you want to go to the
restaurant?   [2]
   b)   Allons à la piscine demain! Let's go to the swimming pool
tomorrow!   [2]
   c)   Tu veux aller à la patinoire avec nous lundi soir? Do you want
to go to the ice-rink with us on Monday night?   [2]
3.   **a)**   Tu veux aller au cinéma demain? Oui, bonne idée! Qu'est-
ce qu'il y a? Il y a Batman, c'est un film de science-fiction.
D'accord. J'adore les films de science-fiction. À quelle heure?
Le film commence à quatre / seize heures.   [5]
   b)   Tu veux aller au cinéma mardi? Oui, bonne idée! Qu'est-
ce qu'il y a? Il y a The Nativity, c'est un film comique.
D'accord. J'adore les films comiques. A quelle heure? Le film
commence à six / dix-huit heures.   [5]

In tests always use what you have in front of you to help construct
your answer. Very often you can re-use words from the question or
activity in your own answer.

Page 49
1.   It is a negative phrase, it adds the word 'never' to the sentence
or phrase.   [1]
2.   **a)**   Je joue à des jeux en ligne.   [1]
   b)   Je fais des recherches.   [1]
   c)   Je fais des achats en ligne.   [1]
3.   Frequency word: souvent, connective: car, intensifier: vraiment,
opinion: amusants   [4]
4.   Any of: Ça m'aide à me détendre, C'est déstressant, On
peut regarder la télé en famille, C'est moins cher que de
sortir.   [4]
5.   Any of: Ça rend accro, On devient mollasson, Il y a trop de
violence, On n'a pas assez d'air frais.   [4]
6.   **a)**   souvent   [1]
   b)   tous les jours   [1]
   c)   rarement   [1]
   d)   le weekend   [1]
   e)   de temps en temps   [1]
   f)   une fois par semaine   [1]

Pages 52–65 Revise Questions

Page 51 Quick Test
1.   Any possible answer from the clothes section of this unit.
2.   The adjective or colour describing the clothing will need to agree
with the gender of the item.
3.   vieux, joli, beau etc.
4.   J'aime cette chemise.

Page 53 Quick Test
1.   Any answer from the chores section of this unit.
2.   Je reçois...par semaine / mois.
3.   Any answer from the saving & spending section of this unit.
4.   Any answer from the part-time jobs section of this unit.

Page 55 Quick Test
1.   **c)**   le musée (masculine)
2.   Pardon, madame, où est la bibliothèque, s'il vous plaît?
3.   I don't like the town because it's too noisy.
4.   **b)**   Il y a beaucoup d'animaux, de fermes et d'arbres et c'est
tranquille.

Page 57 Quick Test
1.   **c)**   au cinéma
2.   Il faut construire plus de magasins au centre-ville.
3.   There are too many banks in the town centre and not enough
restaurants.
4.   **d)**   On peut manger à la banque.

Page 59 Quick Test
1.   France, Espagne and Inde
2.   I often go to the United States.

3.   En France en avion au Portugal en voiture
4.   Normalement je vais en vacances en Italie avec mes parents pour
deux semaines. J'adore l'Italie.

Page 61 Quick Test
1.   En vacances je loge dans une caravane On holiday I stay in a
caravan.
2.   En vacances je me repose et je prends des photos.
3.   Je voudrais réserver une chambre pour deux personnes pour
deux nuits avec un lit double.
4.   La télévision ne marche pas.

Page 63 Quick Test
1.   You must / it is necessary to
2.   Assez, Autant, Beaucoup, Moins, Peu, Plus, Trop.
3.   To give your opinion on an issue: On the one hand... on the other
hand.
4.   Baisser le chauffage
Essayer d'utiliser des produits verts
Éteindre la lumière quand on quitte la pièce
Économiser l'eau
Économiser l'énergie
Utiliser l'énergie solaire

Page 65 Quick Test
1.   Any answer from the current issues section of this unit.
2.   I worry about
3.   Any answer from this unit.
4.   E.g. Respectez la planète!

Pages 66–67 Review Questions

Page 66
1.   **a)**   D   [1]
   b)   E   [1]
   c)   G   [1]
   d)   A   [1]
   e)   F   [1]
2.   **a)**   A   [1]
   b)   A   [1]
   c)   C   [1]
   d)   B   [1]

Page 67
1.   **a)**   un médecin / un infirmier / une infirmière   [1]
   b)   Anyone who works in an office.   [1]
   c)   un directeur / une directrice de magasin   [1]
2.   No need to use un / une   [1]
3.   **a)**   dans quatre ans   [1]
   b)   dans deux ans   [1]
   c)   à l'avenir   [1]
4.   **a)**   Je suis fort(e) en   [1]
   b)   J'ai une passion pour   [1]
   c)   Je ne suis pas interessé(e) par   [1]
5.   Il est **développeur multimédia** et il travaille dans **un bureau**.
Il aime bien son métier car c'est vraiment **motivant** et il peut
créer de nouveaux jeux. Pour être un bon employé il doit être
dynamique.   [5]

Pages 68–69 Review Questions

Page 68
1.   **a)**   le violon   [1]
   b)   la guitare   [1]
   c)   la batterie   [1]
   d)   la trompette   [1]
   e)   le violoncelle   [1]
2.   **a)**   Tu joues du violoncelle.   [1]
   b)   Ma sœur joue de la guitare.   [1]
   c)   Mes frères jouent du piano.   [1]
   d)   Je ne joue pas du violon.   [1]
   e)   Tu joues d'un instrument?   [1]

3. **a)** au [1]
   b) à la [1]
   c) à la [1]
   d) au [1]
   e) à la [1]
4. **a)** préférée, feminine [1]
   b) préfère, verb, I form [1]
   c) préférées, feminine plural [1]
   d) préfères, verb, you form [1]
   e) préféré, masculine [1]
   f) préférés, masculine plural. [1]

Page 69

1. Je ne regarde plus. [2]
2.

English	French	
a cartoon	un dessin animé	
a documentary	un documentaire	
a game show	un jeu télévisé	
a soap	un feuilleton	
a music programme	une émission de musique	
a reality TV programme	une émission de télé-réalité	
the weather forecast	la météo	
the news	les infos	[7]

3. Je regarde la télé de temps en temps. [2]
4. Any of: J'envoie des SMS, Je téléphone à mes amis, Je joue à des jeux, Je fais des recherches en ligne. [3]
5. Any acceptable answer using: Frequency de temps en temps, le weekend, rarement, souvent, tous les jours, une/deux fois par semaine. Opinion amusant, éducatif, marrant, émouvant, nul, effrayant. Quantifier assez, très, vraiment, un peu, trop, plutôt. Connective car, et, mais, parce que. [3]
6. **a)** vraiment [1]
   b) émouvante [1]
   c) éducatif [1]

Pages 70–71 **Practice Questions**

Page 70

1. Je porte un pantalon gris. [3]
2. **a)** Je porte un pull bleu. [1]
   b) Je porte un pantalon blanc. [1]
   c) Je porte une robe verte. [1]
   d) Je porte une chemise jaune. [1]
   e) Je porte des baskets rouges. [1]
3. **a)** Je cherche un pantalon. [1]
   b) Quelle taille? [1]
   c) Quelle couleur? [1]
   d) Ça coute combien? [1]
   e) C'est trop cher. [1]
4. Je reçois 44 euros par mois et j'achète des magazines. [4]

Page 71

1. **a)** G [1]
   b) B [1]
   c) C [1]
   d) F [1]
   e) A [1]
   f) D [1]

2. **a)** country [1]
   b) town [1]
   c) town [1]
   d) country [1]
   e) country [1]
   f) town [1]
3. **a)** true [1]
   b) false [1]
   c) false [1]
   d) true [1]
   e) true [1]
   f) false [1]

In tests when you have lots of parts of questions like these above, answer the parts you are sure about first and go back to the parts you are less sure about. Never leave a blank answer. If you really don't know it is always worth guessing one option or another, e.g. true or false, town or country.

Pages 72–73 **Practice Questions**

Page 72

1. **a)** la Belgique [1]
   b) le Canada [1]
   c) la France [1]
   d) le Portugal [1]
   e) l'Espagne [1]
2. **a)** au Portugal [1]
   b) en Espagne [1]
   c) à Paris [1]
   d) aux États-Unis [1]
3. **a)** normalement [1]
   b) en [1]
   c) parents [1]
   d) dix [1]
   e) avion [1]
   f) hôtel [1]
   g) chaud [1]
   h) dans [1]
4. **a)** je vais [1]
   b) j'ai visité [1]
   c) je loge [1]
   d) je suis resté(e) [1]

Page 73

1. **a)** less [1]
   b) enough [1]
   c) too much/many [1]
2. À mon avis, Selon moi, En ce qui me concerne, Je pense que, Je trouve que, Je crois que [2]
3. **a)** recycle glass [1]
   b) sort the rubbish for recycling [1]
   c) use public transport [1]
   d) protect endangered species [1]
   e) fight global warming [1]
4. Any of: Il faut: Baisser le chauffage, Essayer d'utiliser des produits verts, Éteindre la lumière quand on quitte la pièce, Économiser l'eau, Économiser l'énergie, Utiliser l'énergie solaire. [2]
Il ne faut pas: Détruire la couche d'ozone, Gaspiller l'énergie, Utiliser trop d'emballages, Laisser le robinet ouvert, Laisser la lumière allumée, Utiliser la voiture trop souvent [2]
5. **a)** par contre [1]
   b) selon moi [1]
   c) de l'autre côté [1]
   d) je suis pour [1]
   e) je crois que [1]

Page 75 Quick Test
1. la qualité, le bateau, la fourchette, la nation
2. des chats, des journaux, des tapis, des nez
3. un oiseau, un enfant, un chien, une bougie

Page 77 Quick Test
1. Petite, grande, rouge, grise, curieuse, active
2. adverb, adjective, adjective, adverb, adjective
3. Elle est plus grande **que** moi, Je suis **la moins** timide, Je marche plus vite **que** mon père
4. le meilleur film

Page 79 Quick Test
1. Je suis, nous sommes, mes cheveux sont
2. elle a, elles ont, il a
3. J'ai quatorze ans et ma sœur a seize ans.
4. J'ai soif.

Page 81 Quick Test
1. je regarde, il finit, nous entendons, ils travaillent
2. J'entends, elle adore, nous répondons, nous choisissons
3. Je joue, elle attend, ils / elles regardent, il chante
4. I play or I am playing

Page 83 Quick Test
1. voulez
2. Je ne peux pas faire mes devoirs..
3. At school, we must not (one must not) wear jeans.
4. **b)** Il ne peut pas travailler. It's negative and in the il form.

Page 85 Quick Test
1. They are doing their maths homework but they are not going to finish their English homework.
2. Je vais regarder la télévision.
3. **b)** allez
4. **c)** Je fais du shopping.

Page 87 Quick Test
1. She wakes up, she gets up, has a shower and gets dressed in her room.
2. Il se lève à six heures et il se couche à neuf heures et demie.
3. **a)** fais
   b) écoute
   c) mange
4. **a)** allez
   b) finissez
   c) dansez

Page 89 Quick Test
1. She saw the film but she didn't eat popcorn.
2. J'ai joué au football, j'ai regardé la télé et j'ai fini mes devoirs.
3. **a)** j'ai fait
   b) j'ai écouté
   c) j'ai bu
4. **a)** elle est allée
   b) elle est restée
   c) elle est sortie

Page 90
1. un pull, un jean, des chaussures / des baskets [3]
2. **a)** cotton [1]
   b) leather [1]
   c) wool [1]
3. Je porte un joli chapeau. [1]
4. Any of: Je fais les courses, Je fais la cuisine, Je fais la vaisselle, Je garde mon petit-frère, Je lave la voiture, Je mets la table, Je passe l'aspirateur, Je promène le chien, Je range ma chambre, Je sors la poubelle, Je travaille dans le jardin. [3]
5. Possible starters + any suitable reason: J'économise, Je fais des économies pour, J'achète… [4]
6. **a)** une robe bleue [1]
   b) un pull blanc [1]
   c) une jupe verte [1]
   d) des chausseurs noires [1]

Page 91
1. **a)** B le marché [1]
   b) A le magasin [1]
   c) A le centre commercial [1]
   d) A la boulangerie [1]
2. **a)** C à la piscine [1]
   b) B au restaurant [1]
   c) A à la gare [1]
   d) A au parc [1]
3. **a)** C [1]
   b) A [1]
   c) B [1]

Page 92
1. **a)** La France [1]
   b) Le Portugal [1]
   c) L'Italie [1]
   d) L'Écosse [1]
   e) L'Angleterre [1]
   f) L'Espagne [1]

Note le / la becomes l' when the following noun starts with a vowel.

2. **a)** en Italie (feminine) [1]
   b) en France (feminine) [1]
   c) aux États-Unis (plural) [1]
   d) en Inde (feminine) [1]
   e) en Afrique (feminine) [1]
3. **David**: Je passe mes vacances aux États-Unis avec mes grands-parents pendant deux semaines. Je voyage en avion. Je loge dans un hôtel et je me relaxe. [5]
   Marcel: Je passe mes vacances en France avec mes parents pendant sept jours. Je voyage en voiture. Je loge dans un camping et je vais à la plage. [5]
4. **a)** Où vas–tu en vacances? Tu vas où en vacances? [1]
   b) Avec qui y vas-tu? Tu y vas avec qui? [1]
   c) Où restes-tu? Tu restes où? [1]
   d) Qu'est-ce que tu fais en vacances normalement? Tu fais quoi normalement? [1]

Page 93

1.

French	English
Agissez!	Do something/take action!
Conservez!	Conserve!
Évitez!	Avoid!
Jetez!	Throw!
Protégez!	Protect
Réduisez!	Reduce!
Respectez!	Respect!
Sauvez!	Save!

[7]

2. To explain how much or how many: e.g. assez, autant, beaucoup, moins, peu, plus, trop. [2]
3. **a)** bruit, circulation, criminalité, pollution [1]
   b) travail, espaces verts [1]
4. Any two of the global issues listed on pages 70–71 [2]
5. **a)** utiliser [1]
   b) recycler [1]
   c) protéger [1]

Pages 94–95 **Practice Questions**

Page 94
1. **a)** la [1]
   b) le [1]
   c) la [1]
   d) la [1]
   e) les [1]
   f) la [1]
   g) le [1]
   h) les [1]
   i) la [1]
   j) les [1]
2. **a)** des maisons blanches [1]
   b) des chiens noirs [1]
   c) des souris grises [1]
   d) des chevaux marron [1]
   e) des chats roux [1]
3. **a)** petite [1]
   b) timide [1]
   c) sportifs [1]
   d) marron [1]
   e) grande [1]
4. **a)** J'ai les cheveux marron/bruns. [1]
   b) J'habite dans une maison blanche. [1]
   c) Ma sœur est grande. [1]
   d) J'ai une petite souris grise. [1]
   e) Mark est plus grand que Léo. [1]

Page 95
1. **a)** nous avons [1]
   b) je suis [1]
   c) tu as [1]
   d) vous êtes [1]
   e) Mes sœurs ont [1]
2. **a)** tu joues [1]
   b) Mes sœurs s'appellent [1]
   c) je finis [1]

d) elle attend [1]
e) vous aimez [1]
3. **a)** Il y a [1]
   b) c'est [1]
   c) Il y a [1]
   d) Il n'y a pas de [1]
   e) Il y a [1]
4. **a)** J'ai froid. [1]
   b) Ma sœur a quinze ans. [1]
   c) Tu as soif? [1]
   d) Ils ont très chaud. [1]
   e) Quel âge ont-ils? [1]

All of the examples in question 4 above use **avoir** (to have) in French where in English we use the verb to be.

5. **a)** je regarde [1]
   b) elle attend [1]
   c) nous aimons [1]
   d) je joue [1]
   e) ils mangent [1]

Pages 96–97 **Practice Questions**

Page 96
1. **a)** je veux [1]
   b) tu peux [1]
   c) elle doit [1]
   d) ells veulent [1]
   e) nous devons [1]
   f) vous pouvez [1]
2. **a)** tu fais [1]
   b) il fait [1]
   c) Qu'est-ce que vous faites [1]
   d) ils font [1]
   e) je fais [1]
3. **a)** Je vais regarder la télé. [1]
   b) Tu vas écouter de la musique? [1]
   c) Il va jouer au foot. [1]
   d) Nous allons aller au parc. [1]
   e) Est-ce que vous allez travailler? [1]
   f) Les filles vont faire du shopping. [1]

Page 97
1. **a)** fermez [1]
   b) ouvrez [1]
   c) mange [1]
   d) fais [1]
   e) écoutez [1]
   f) regarde [1]
2. **a)** m' [1]
   b) se [1]
   c) te [1]
   d) s' [1]
   e) vous [1]
3. **a)** J'ai mangé beaucoup de pommes. [1]
   b) Je suis allé(e) au club des jeunes. [1]
   c) J'ai regardé le match de foot. [1]
   d) Je suis arrivé(e) en retard. [1]
   e) J'ai fini mes devoirs. [1]
   f) J'ai fait de la natation. [1]
   g) Je suis sorti(e) avec mes amis. [1]
   h) J'ai dansé avec Paul. [1]

Pages 98–105 **Revise Questions**

Page 99 Quick Test
1. For regular verbs it is the infinitive. For irregular verbs it varies.
2. Vouloir, pouvoir, devoir, boire, prendre etc.

3. ai, as, a, ons, ez, ont
4. we will have
5. elle finira

Page 101 Quick Test
1. A noun
2. Yes, the pronoun would change (eg. le / la).
3. It is an indirect pronoun so replaces a noun that is linked to the verbs by the word à.
4. y

Page 103 Quick Test
1. The nous form of the present tense with the 'ons' ending removed.
2. To describe:
   something you used to do.
   a repeated action in the past.
   a description of the past, e.g. weather and opinions.
3. true
4. ais, ait, ions, iez, aient
5. nous visitions

Page 105 Quick Test
1. Future stem + imperfect ending.
2. If I played the match, I would win the competition.
3. Le sandwich a été mangé par Carla. The sandwich was eaten by Carla.
4. The film was seen by Simone.

Page 106
1. a) The stem (for regular verbs this is the infinitive) [1]
   b) The ending (the ending changes depending on the subject of the verb) [1]
2. The immediate future is used for events that are going to take place in the close future whereas the future tense can be extended to longer term. E.g Immediate future - Je vais jouer – I am going to play, future tense – Je jouerai – I will play [3]
3. Y [1]
4. Any 3 of: toi, lui, elle, soi, nous, vous, eux, elles [3]
5. Je la mange [1]
6. a) Je jouerai [1]
   b) Elle finira [1]
   c) Nous apprendrons [1]

Page 107
1. Perfect tense because it is a single action in the past [2]
2. To describe something that you would do [2]
3. a) jouais [1]
   b) allait [1]
   c) étions [1]
4. Le gâteau est mangé par Carla. [2]
5. If I was rich I would buy a castle. j'étais imperfect, j'achéterais conditional [3]
6. Louise est détestée par Simon. [1]

Page 108
1. a) une mère [1]
   b) une fille [1]
   c) des enfants [1]
   d) un bateau [1]
   e) des chiens [1]
   f) un jardin [1]
   g) une maison [1]
   h) un ordinateur [1]
   i) des tables [1]
   j) une souris [1]
2. a) petite [1]
   b) blanc [1]
   c) rouges [1]
   d) mon [1]
   e) mes [1]
   f) bruns [1]
3. a) J'ai une souris grise. [1]
   b) Nous avons un gros chien noir. [1]
   c) Ma sœur a une tortue. [1]
   d) Je n'aime pas les grosses souris. [1]
   e) J'ai un petit chien blanc. [1]
4. a) J'ai un chat marron. (masculine) [1]
   b) J'habite dans une petite maison. (feminine) [1]
   c) Ma sœur a les yeux marron. (plural but marron never changes) [1]
   d) Ma chambre est grande et bleue. (feminine) [1]
   e) Mes chats sont petits et blancs. (masculine plural) [1]
5. Bonjour je m'appelle Anna.J'ai **les yeux bleus** et je suis **grande**. J'ai **deux sœurs**. J'habite dans **une grande maison blanche**. J'ai **deux chiens blancs** et **deux petites souris grises** [6]

Page 109
1. a) nous avons [1]
   b) mes sœurs ont [1]
   c) tu as [1]
   d) j'ai [1]
   e) mon père a [1]
2. a) ma sœur est [1]
   b) je suis [1]
   c) mon lit est [1]
   d) où sont [1]
   e) les cheveux de ma mère sont [1]
3. a) Nous finissons tous les jours à 15.30. [1]
   b) Vous attendez qui? [1]
   c) Tu aimes le chocolat? [1]
   d) Elle travaille bien à l'école. [1]
   e) Mes sœurs regardent souvent la télé. [1]
4. a) Ma mère a 45 ans. [1]
   b) Mes sœurs ont 10 et 13 ans. [1]
   c) J'ai faim. [1]
   d) Tu as soif? As-tu soif? Est-ce que tu as soif? [1]
   e) Nous avons froid. [1]
5. a) I play [1]
   b) What are you doing / I am revising [2]
   c) I travel / we are travelling [2]
   d) I listen or I am listening [1]

Page 110
1. a) veux [1]
   b) peuvent [1]
   c) devons [1]
   d) veut [1]
   e) peut [1]
   f) dois [1]
2. a) ii faire du shopping. [1]
   b) ii fait chaud. [1]
   c) iii faire de la natation. [1]
3. a) je vais nager [1]
   b) je vais danser [1]
   c) Je vais regarder un film [1]
   d) je vais aller à la pêche [1]

Page 111

1. a) C mangez [1]
   b) A bois [1]
   c) C finissez [1]
   d) A sors [1]
   e) B regarde [1]
2. a) A à sept heures [1]
   b) B dans la salle de bains [1]
   c) C les mains [1]
   d) C tu te couches? [1]
3. a) J'ai mangé une banane. [1]
   b) Nous avons parlé à son frère. [1]
   c) Ils ont bu du café. [1]
   d) Elle est arrivée en retard. [1]
   e) Les deux filles sont allées au centre commercial. [1]
   f) Est-ce que tu as fini tes devoirs? [1]
   g) Les garçons sont sortis avec leurs amis. [1]
   h) Vous avez vu le film? [1]

Pages 112–113 **Review Questions**

Page 112

1. False, the infinitive is not used for irregular verbs. [1]
2. To emphasize a subject pronoun, as a one word answer to a question or after prepositions. [1]
3. en [1]
4. Elle les aide. [1]
5.

Infinitive	Stem	Future tense phrase
regarder	regarder	il regardera
manger	manger	je mangerai
finir	finir	tu finiras
vendre	vendr	ils vendront
faire	fer	nous ferons
avoir	aur	elle aura
aller	ir	vous irez

[12]

6. a) subject [1]
   b) emphatic [1]
   c) direct object [1]

Page 113

1. To describe what you used to do, a repeated action in the past or to describe something in the past. [2]
2.

Subject	Ending	Conjugation of Visiter
je	ais	je visitais
tu	ais	tu visitais
il	ait	il visitait
nous	ions	nous visitions
vous	iez	vous visitiez
elles	aient	elles visitaient

[10]

3. Nous écouterions la radio. conditional [1]
4. a) Il mangerait de la pizza. [1]
   b) Vous perdriez la competition. [1]
5. a) The book is read by Élodie. [1]
   b) Élodie lit le livre. [1]

Pages 114–125 **Mixed Test-Style Questions**

1. a, f, h, g, i, b, c, e, d [8]
2. a) Lena [1]
   b) Christelle [1]
   c) Christelle [1]
   d) Lena [1]
   e) Lena [1]

With complex reading tasks like 1 and 2 above, it is always a good idea to read all the way through first, including all the questions, to get the gist of what the text is about and what you are looking for, then read again more slowly while you work out your answers.

3. a) dix [1]
   b) trois [1]
   c) partage [1]
   d) une télévision [1]
   e) génial [1]
4. a) ice rink [1]
   b) on Tuesday [1]
   c) in front of the sports centre [2]
   d) 2 p.m. [1]
5. a) false [1]
   b) false [1]
   c) false [1]
   d) true [1]
   e) true [1]
   f) false [1]
6. a) une glace à la fraise [1]
   b) un thé au citron [1]
   c) un gateau au café [1]
   d) un sandwich au jambon [1]
   e) une tarte aux abricots [1]
   f) un café au lait [1]
   g) une mousse au chocolat [1]
   h) la soupe de poisson [1]

Use grammar to help you work out your answers. For example 'une glace à la' has to match with 'fraise' because that is the only feminine singular word in the list of options. Grammar is a key to getting good marks!

7. a) Salma [1]
   b) Chantal [1]
   c) Oscar [1]
   d) Salma [1]
   e) Salma [1]
   f) Chantal [1]
   g) Oscar [1]
8. a) l'histoire [1]
   b) la géographie [1]
   c) la musique [1]
   d) la biologie [1]
   e) l'informatique [1]
   f) le français [1]
   g) le sport / l'EPS [1]
9. a) positive [1]
   b) negative [1]
   c) negative [1]
   d) negative [1]
   e) positive [1]

f) negative [1]
g) positive [1]
h) negative [1]
10. Suggested answers
   a) Mon collège s'appelle….. [1]
   b) Il se trouve à… [1]
   c) Il y a ….élèves. [1]
   d) Les cours commencent à…. [1]
   e) Je parle avec mes amis / je joue au foot / je mange des biscuits. [1]
   f) Je porte un pantalon noir, une chemise blanche… [1]
   g) Je préfère…. [1]
   h) Les cours finissent à… [1]
11. a) rugby [1]
   b) tennis [1]
   c) swimming [1]
   d) football [1]
   e) golf [1]
12. a) Je ne veux pas manger; j'ai mal à l'estomac. [1]
   b) Je ne peux pas faire une promenade; j'ai mal aux pieds. [1]
   c) Je veux une aspirine; j'ai mal à la tête. [1]
   d) Je vais chez le dentiste; j'ai mal aux dents. [1]
   e) Je ne peux pas faire mes devoirs; j'ai mal à la main. [1]
   f) Je ne peux pas parler; j'ai mal à la gorge. [1]
13. a) Les fruits et les légumes sont bons pour la santé. [1]
   b) Au petit-déjeuner, je bois du chocolat / thé / café chaud. [1]
   c) Mon légume préféré, c'est le chou. [1]
   d) Il faut boire beaucoup d'eau. [1]
   e) Il ne faut pas fumer de cigarettes. [1]
14. Je travaille comme pilote parce que c'est très passionnant. [5]
15. a) nurse [1]
   b) footballer because it's well paid and stimulating [1]
16. au collège, examens, va, les sciences, être [1]
17. b, e, a, d, c [1]
18. a) Tuesday 1.25am / pm [1]
   b) Wednesday 1.15pm [1]
   c) Sunday, midday, 12.00pm [1]
   d) Monday 3.30pm [1]
   e) Thursday 5.45pm [1]
19. a) B [1]
   b) A [1]
   c) C [1]
   d) D [1]
20. a) 2 [1]
   b) 5 [1]
   c) 2 [1]
   d) It's included in the price. [1]
   e) 268 Euros [1]

21. Students' own answers [4]
22. Students' own answers [6]
23. il écoutera; elles choisiront; nous perdrons [3]
24. a) global warming and climate change; [2]
   b) everyone; [1]
   c) recycle or sort rubbish for recycling; use public transport [2]
   d) use; sort; do [3]
25. the infinitive [1]
26. assez, plus, trop, beaucoup [4]
27. any of the following: souvent, tous les jours, le weekend, parfois; beaucoup, bien; car, parce que; plus an opinion. [4]
28. a) La banque [1]
   b) La gare [1]
   c) La bibliothèque [1]
   d) Le centre commercial / le marché / les magasins [1]
29. a) Ma ville est animée et il y a beaucoup de faire. [1]
   b) Ma ville est très calme et tranquille. [1]
   c) L'air est sale et pollué. [1]
   d) Le marché est excellent si on veut acheter des fruits. [1]
   e) Il y a beaucoup de cafés et de restaurants. [1]
   f) Il ya trop de voitures au centre-ville. [1]
   g) Le jardin public est joli. [1]
   h) Il n'y a pas assez de magasins. [1]
30. Suggested answers
   a) le musée, les monuments, l'église. [1]
   b) c'est animé [1]
   c) le cinéma, le théâtre [1]
   d) le stade, le centre de loisirs [1]
   e) le centre commercial [1]
31. d; c; b; e; a [5]
32. a) j'ai regardé [1]
   b) tu as bu [1]
   c) il a ecouté [1]
   d) nous avons travaillé [1]
   e) elle a fini [1]
   f) les deux garçons ont vu [1]
   g) vous avez fait [1]
   h) j'ai dansé [1]

Glossary

Family

à, *prep*, at / in / to

agaçant(e), *adj*, annoying

anglais(e), *adj*, English

anniversaire, *nm*, birthday

beau-père, *nm*, step-dad

belle-mère, *nf*, step-mum

cheveux, *npl*, hair

chat, *nm*, cat

chien, *nm*, dog

court(e), *adj*, short

demi-frère, *nm*, step or half brother

demi-sœur, *nf*, step or half sister

famille, *nf*, family

fille unique, *nf*, only child

fils unique, *nm*, only child

français(e), *adj*, French

frisé, *adj*, curly

gros (grosse), *adj*, fat / big

jumeau (jumelle), *adj*, twin

mignon (mignonne), *adj*, cute

mince, *adj*, slim

oiseau, *nm*, bird

paresseux (paresseuse), *adj*, lazy

poisson, *nm*, fish

quand, *adv*, when

raide, *adj*, straight

roux (rousse), *adj*, ginger

souris, *nf*, mouse

sympathique, *adj*, friendly / nice

tante, *nf*, aunt

timide, *adj*, shy

yeux (oeil), *npl / nm*, eyes (eye)

House and Home

Angleterre, *nf*, England

armoire, *nf*, wardrobe

appartement, *nm*, flat

bord de mer, *nm*, seaside

campagne, *nf*, countryside

canapé, *nm*, sofa

chaise, *nf*, chair

chambre, *nf*, bedroom

cuisine, *nf*, kitchen

chez, *prep*, at / in / to someone's

dans, *prep*, in

derrière, *prep*, behind

devant, *prep*, in front of

France, *nf*, France

jardin, *nm*, garden

lit, *nm*, bed

loin, *prep*, far

maison, *nf*, house

nord, *nm*, north

où, *adv*, where

partager, *vb*, to share

pièce, *nf*, a room

près, *prep*, near

salle à manger, *nf*, dining room

salle de bains, *nf*, bathroom

salon, *nm*, living room

sud, *nm*, south

sur, *prep*, on

Royaume-Uni, *nm*, United Kingdom

toilettes, *npl*, toilet

ville, *nf*, town

Food and Drink

banane, *nf*, banana

boire, *vb*, to drink

café au lait, *nm*, white coffee

carotte, *nf*, carrot

champignon, *nm*, mushroom

chocolat chaud, *nm*, hot chocolate

chou, *nm*, cabbage

chou-fleur, *nm*, cauliflower

citron, *nm*, lemon

coca, *nm*, coke

de temps en temps, *adv*, from time to time

eau minérale, *nf*, a mineral water

fraise, *nf*, strawberry

fruit, *nm*, a fruit

des fruits de mer, *nm*, sea food

glace, *nf*, an ice cream

des haricots verts, *nm*, green beans

jus d'orange, *nm*, an orange juice

légume, *nm*, a vegetable

limonade, *nf*, lemonade

manger, *vb*, to eat

oignon, *nm*, onion

des petits pois, *nm*, peas

pêche, *nf*, peach

poire, *nf*, pear

du poisson, *nm*, fish

pomme, *nf*, apple

pomme de terre, *nf*, potato

du poulet, *nf*, chicken

quelquefois, *adv*, sometimes

sandwich au fromage, *nm*, a cheese sandwich

sandwich au jambon, *nm*, a ham sandwich

souvent, *adv*, often

rarement, *adv*, rarely

thé au citron, *nm*, lemon tea

tous les jours, *adv*, every day

Sport and Health

badminton, *nm*, badminton

basket, *nm*, basketball

billard, *nm*, billiards

bras, *nm*, arm

cartes, *nf*, cards

dentiste, *nm*, a dentist

dents, *nf*, teeth

dos, *nm*, back

échecs, *nm*, chess

enrhumé, *adj*, havng a cold

l'équitation, *nf*, horse-riding

estomac, *nf*, stomach

football, *nm*, football

fumer, *vb*, to smoke

gorge, *nf*, throat

grippe, *nf*, flu

hôpital, *nm*, hospital

jambe, *nf*, leg

jeux de société, *nm*, board games

jouer, *vb*, to play

malade, *adj*, ill

médecin, *nm*, a doctor

mini-golf, *nm*, crazy golf

de natation, *nf*, swimming

oreilles, *nf*, ears

du patinage, *nm*, skating

pétanque, *nf*, French bowls

pharmacie, *nf*, the chemist

pied, *nm*, foot

rendez-vous, *nm*, appointment

rugby, *nm*, rugby

du ski, *nm*, skiing

tennis, *nm*, tennis

tennis de table, *nm*, table tennis

tête, *nf*, head

du vélo, *nm*, cycling

yeux, *nm*, eyes

School and Education

allemand, *nm*, German

amusant, *adj*, fun

anglais, *nm*, English

bâtiment, *nm*, building

bibliothèque, *nf*, library

biologie, *nf*, biology

cantine, *nf*, canteen

chimie, *nm*, chemistry

commencer, *vb*, to start

cours, *nm*, lesson

dessin, *nm*, art

difficile, *adj*, difficult

dur, *adj*, hard

éducation physique et sportive, *nf*, PE

élève, *nm / f*, pupil

ennuyeux, *adj*, boring

espagnol, *nm*, Spanish

facile, *adj*, easy

finir, *vb*, to end

français, *nm*, French

géographie, *nf*, geography

histoire, *nf*, history

informatique, *nf*, IT

instruction religieuse, *nf*, religious studies

intéressant, *adj*, interesting

inutile, *adj*, useless

maths, *nm*, maths

musique, *nf*, music

nul, *adj*, rubbish

pause-déjeuner, *nf*, lunch break

physique, *nf*, physics

professeur, *nm*, teacher

récréation, *nf*, break

sciences, *nf*, science

super, *adj*, great

technologie, *nf*, technology

terrain de sport, *nm*, a playground

uniforme scolaire, *nm*, school uniform

utile, *adj*, useful

Future Plans

avocat(e), *nm / f*, lawyer

bien payé(e), *adj*, well-paid

chanteur / chanteuse, *nm / f*, singer

coiffeur / coiffeuse, *nm / f*, hairdresser

communiquer, *vb*, to communicate

coopérer, *vb*, to cooperate

créer, *vb*, to create

développeur / développeuse multimédia, *nm / f*, video game designer

directeur / directrice de magasin, *nm / f*, shop manager

dynamique, *adj*, energetic

étudier, *vb*, study

footballeur, *nm / f*, footballer

frustrant(e), *adj*, frustrating

gagner, *vb*, earn

gratifiant(e), *adj*, rewarding

infirmier / infirmière, *nm / f*, nurse

ingénieur(e), *nm / f*, engineer

journaliste, *nm / f*, journalist

médecin, *nm / f*, doctor

motivant(e), *adj*, motivating

organisé(e), *adj*, organised

partager, *vb*, to share

passionné(e), *adj*, passionate

patient(e), *adj*, patient

pilote, *nm / f*, pilot

poli(e), *adj*, polite

professeur, *nm / f*, teacher

respectueux / respectueuse, *adj*, respectful

travailleur / travailleuse, *adj*, hardworking

travailler, *vb*, work

vétérinaire, *nm / f*, vet

Leisure

aimer, *vb*, to like

aller, *vb*, to go

allons, *vb*, let's go

barbant(e), *adj*, boring

batterie, *nf*, drums

bibliothèque, *nf*, library

centre sportif, *nm*, sports centre

comédie, *nf*, a comedy

concert, *nm*, concert

détester, *vb*, to hate

dessin animé, *nm*, cartoon

écouter, *adj*, to listen

ennuyeux (ennuyeuse), *adj*, boring

entraînant(e), *adj*, lively

film d'amour / de science-fiction, *nm*, romance / sci-fi film

flim historique, *nm*, historical film

film d'horreur, *nm*, horror film

groupe, *nm*, band

guitare, *nf*, guitar

jouer à+instrument, *vb*, to play an instrument

lecteur MP3, *nm*, MP3 player

musique classique / pop, *nf*, classical / pop music

patinoire, *nf*, ice rink

piscine, *nf*, swimming pool

préféré(e), *adj*, favourite

préférer, *vb*, to prefer

relaxant(e), *adj*, relaxing

violon, *nm*, violin

violoncelle, *nm*, cello

TV and Technology

assez, *adv*, quite

comédie, *nf*, comedy

documentaire, *nm*, documentary

éducatif(ive), *adj*, educational

effrayant(e), *adj*, scary

émission de télé-réalité, *nf*, reality TV programme

émouvant(e) , *adj*, moving

envoyer, *vb*, to send

feuilleton, *nm*, soap opera

film, *nm*, film

infos, *nm*, the news

jeu télévisé, *nm*, game show

météo, *nf*, the weather forecast

ne... pas, *adv*, not

ne... jamais, *adv*, never

ne... plus, *adv*, no longer

ne... que, *adv*, only

peu, *adv*, a bit

plutôt, *adv*, rather

rarement, *adv*, rarely

regarder, *vb*, watch

série, *nf*, a series

souvent, *adv*, often

tchatter, *vb*, online chat

télécharger, *vb*, download

très, *adv*, very

trop, *adv*, too

vraiment, *nm*, really

weekend, *nm*, weekend

Shopping and Money

à la mode, *adj*, fashionable / trendy

acheter, *vb*, to buy

baby-sitting, *nm*, babysitting

baskets, *npl*, trainers

chausettes, *npl*, socks

chaussures, *npl*, shoes

chapeau, *nm*, hat

collant, *nm*, tights

chemise, *nf*, shirt

cool, *adj*, cool

cravate, *nf*, tie

demodé(e), *adj*, old-fashioned

économiser, *vb*, save

garder, *vb*, look after

jean, *nm*, jeans

jogging, *nm*, jogging bottoms

lunettes, *npl*, glasses

jupe, *nf*, skirt

manteau, *nm*, coat

moche, *adj*, ugly

pantalon, *nm*, trousers

petit boulot, *nm*, part-time job

pull, *nm*, jumper

rayé, *adj*, stripy

recevoir, *vb*, receive

robe, *nf*, dress

sweat à capuche, *nm*, hoodie

t-shirt, *nm*, t-shirt

véste, *nf*, jacket

Where I Live

animé, *adj*, lively
assez de, *adv*, enough
banlieue, *nf*, suburb
banque, *nf*, bank
beaucoup de, *adv*, a lot of
bruyant, *adj*, noisy
campagne, *nf*, countryside
centre commercial, *nm*, shopping centre
centre de loisirs, *nm*, the leisure centre
centre-ville, *nm*, the town centre
construire, *vb*, to build
continuer, *vb*, to carry on, continue
créer, *vb*, to create
église, *nf*, church
ennuyeux, *adj*, boring
gare, *nf*, station
habiter, *nm*, to live
hôtel de ville, *nm*, the town hall
industriel, *adj*, industrial
jardin public, *nm*, park
loin de, *prep*, a long way from
magasin, *nm*, shop
marché, *nm*, the market
musée, *nm*, the museum
piscine, *nf*, the swimming pool
pollué, *adj*, polluted
prendre, *vb*, to take
près de, *prep*, near
propre, *adj*, clean
tourner, *vb*, to turn
tranquille, *adj*, quiet
trop de, *adv*, too much
village, *nm*, village
ville, *nf*, town, city
voir, *vb*, to see
zone piétonne, *nf*, pedestrian zone

Holidays

au, *prep*, to / in the + masculine countries / masculine places
auberge de jeunesse, *nf*, youth hostel
aux, *prep*, to / in the + plural countries
avion, *nm*, plane
avec, *prep*, with
avec qui, *prep*, who with
balcon, *nm*, balcony
bateau, *nm*, boat
bruyant , *adj*, noisy
camping, *nm*, campsite
camping-car, *nm*, campervan
une caravane, *nf*, caravan
cassé(e), *adj*, broken
combien, *adv*, how much / many
douche, *nf*, shower
en, *prep*, by + means of transport
États-Unis, *npl*, Unites States
faire des courses, *vb*, to shop
Grande Bretagne, *nf*, Great Britain
Inde, *nf*, India
montagne, *nf*, mountain
nuit, *nf*, night
pays, *nm*, country
plage, *nf*, beach
rester, *vb*, to stay
sale, *adj*, dirty
sans, *prep*, without
tente, *nf*, a tent
vacances, *npl*, holidays
vélo, *nm*, bike
visiter, *vb*, to visit
voiture, *nf*, car
voyager, *vb*, to travel
y, *prep*, there

Global Issues

agir, *vb*, to take action

assez, *adv*, enough

autant, *adv*, as much / as many

beaucoup, *adv*, a lot / many

conserver, *vb*, to conserve

cruauté, *nf*, cruelty

déforestation, *nf*, deforestation

éviter, *vb*, to avoid

essayer, *vb*, try

énergie, *nf*, energy

faim, *nf*, hunger

guerre, *nf*, war

lutter, *vb*, to fight

jeter, *vb*, to throw

moins, *adv*, less

pauvreté, *nf*, poverty

penser, *vb*, to think

peu, *adv*, few / little

plus, *adv*, more

pollution, *nf*, pollution

protéger, *vb*, to protect

recycler, *vb*, to recycle

réchauffement de la planète, *nm*, global warming

recyclage, *nm*, recycling

réduiser, *vb*, to reduce

respecter, *vb*, to respect

sauver, *vb*, to save

soutenir, *vb*, to support

terrorisme, *nm*, terrorism

trop, *adv*, too much / too many

trouver, *vb*, to find

Index

accommodation 60
à côté de (near) 10
adjectives 76–7
    after / before noun 50–1
    agreeing with noun 39
    family 6, 7
    leisure 35
    work 31
à droite (to the right) 55
adverbs 62, 76–7
à gauche (to the left) 55
age 4
à (in) 8
    see also au / aux, à ...
à la / au / à l' / aux 18, 36
aller (to go) 33, 37, 84–5
ambitions 33
à mon avis (in my opinion) 63
arrangements 37
asking questions 4
assez (quite) 7
attendre (to wait) 81
at the 36
au / aux (to / in + countries) 59
auxiliaries 78
avez-vous? (have you?) 15
avoir (to have) 78–9, 88

bad for you 18
best fit translation 63
brand names 40

café au lait (white coffee) 12
ça m'aide à (it helps me to) 41
ça me plait (I like it / that) 17, 35
c'est bon pour la santé (it's healthy) 19
c'est / ce sont (it is) 27, 32, 64, 79
c'est mauvais pour la santé
(it's unhealthy) 19
chanter (to sing) 80
chez (at / to someone's) 9, 37
chores 11, 52–3
cinema 37
clothes 50
colours 29, 50
combattre (to fight) 65
comparatives 77
complaints 61
conditional tense 104–5
consonants ending words 5, 82
continuer (to continue) 33
countries 58–9
country vs town 55

courses, meals 14
current issues 64

dans (in) 8
day at school 28
de (a / any) 10–11, 52
descriptions 50–1
desserts 14
de temps en temps (from time to time)
13, 39
devoir (to have to / must) 83
directions 55
dislikes 13, 16, 26–7, 35, 39
dos / don'ts 62
drink 12–15
du / de la / de l', des (some) 10, 52

education 26–9
elle (she) 7, 9
energy 63
en (to / in) 8, 59
–er verbs 80–1
est-ce qu'il y a (is / are there?) 61
être (to be) 78–9, 89
étudier (to study) 33
eyes 6
faire (to do / make) 17, 33, 84–5
family 4–7
favourites 35
feminine nouns 9, 58, 74
finir (to finish) 81
first course 14
food 12–15
fruits 12
future
    immediate 84–5
    plans 30–3
    tense 33, 84–5, 98–9

games 16, 40–1
gender 50, 74–5
global issues 62–5
good for you 18
hair 6
health 16–19
    feeling unwell 18
    getting help 19
    good / bad for you 18
    staying healthy 19
holidays 58–61
home 8–11
    inside my 9
    items in 10

    where I live 8
    where things are 10
house 8–11
how often 11, 13, 16, 39

il faut (you must) 57, 63
il (he) 7, 9
–ille, word ending 54
il ne faut pas (you must not) 63
il n'y a pas (there isn't) 9, 57
il y a (there is) 5, 28, 57, 79
immediate future 84–5, 98
imperative 65, 86–7
imperfect tense 102–3
impersonal pronouns 101
infinitive form of verb 60
information about others 5
internet 40
irregular verbs 99
    avoir / être 78–9, 88, 89
    future tense 104
–ir verbs 80–1

j'achète (I buy) 53
j'adore (I love) 27
j'ai... ans (I am... years old) 5
j'ai choisi (I've chosen) 15
j'ai horreur de (I really hate) 17
j'ai mal... (I've got a sore...) 19
j'aime (I like) 27
je bois (I drink) 13
je déteste (I hate) 27
je fais (I do) 11, 53
je mange (I eat) 13
je m'appelle (my name is) 5
je me passionne pour (I really love) 17
je m'intéresse à (I'm interested in) 17
je n'aime pas (I don't like) 27
je n'ai pas (I don't have) 5, 11
je ne peux pas supporter (I can't stand) 17
je prends (I'll have) 15
je reçois (I receive) 53
j'espère (I hope) 31
je suis (I am) 5
je suis malade (I'm ill) 19
je travaille (I work) 53
je vais (I go) 59
je veux (I want) 31
je voudrais (I'd like) 13, 15, 31, 61
j'habite (I live) 9
jobs 30, 53
jouer (to play) 16, 34, 35
j'y vais (I go there) 59

la / le / l' / les 10, 18, 26, 36, 52
leisure 34–7
le / la / l' / les 10, 18, 26, 36, 52
les cheveux (hair) 7
les yeux (eyes) 7
likes 13, 16, 26–7, 35, 39
living places 4, 8, 54–7
location 8–9
loin de (far from) 55

main course 14
marron (brown) 6
masculine nouns 9, 58, 74
meals 14
meilleur (better) 19
members of family 5
mieux (better) 19
mobile phones 40
modal verbs 31, 82–3
moins de (less) 19, 57
money 50–3
MRS VAN DER TRAMP mnemonic 89
music 34–5

names 4–5
negatives 11, 83, 85, 88
ne... jamais (never) 39
ne... plus (no longer) 39
nouns 9, 39, 58, 74

object of sentence 105
often see how often
on ne peut pas (you can't) 57
on (one / we / you) 41
on peut (you can) 41, 57
on va? (shall we go?) 37
opinions 27, 39, 62
ordering food 12, 14
others 5
où est...? (where is...?) 55

parce que (because) 27, 35
part-time jobs 53
pas de (aren't) 9
passive voice 104–5
past participles 88–9
perfect tense 88–9, 102
personality 7
personal pronouns 100–1
pets 7
phones 40
places 36, 54
plurals 74–5
plus de (more) 57

pocket money 52
polite form of verb 14
pouvoir (to be able to / can) 82
préféré (favourite) 35
prepositions 8
près de (near) 55
present tense 81
priorities 32, 64
problems 64–5
programmes on TV 38
pronouns 100–1
pronunciation
    –ais / aient endings 102
    consonants ending words 5, 75, 82
    guide 126
    h and i 37
    holiday words 61
    –ille endings 54
protéger (to protect) 65

quantifiers 7
quantity 15, 62
quelquefois (sometimes) 13
questions 4
quitter (to leave) 33

rarement (rarely) 13
reasons why 27, 33
recipes 15
recycler (to recycle) 65
reflexive pronouns 101
reflexive verbs 86–7
regarder (to watch) 38
regular verbs 80–1, 104
reservations 61
respecter (to respect) 65
–re verbs 80–1, 98
rules at school 29

sandwich fillings 12
s'appelle (is called) 7
saving 52
school 26–9
selon moi (in my opinion) 63
servez-vous? (do you serve?) 14
shopping 50–3
sickness 18
si clauses 104
size 6
social networking 40
some 15, 52
souvent (often) 13, 39
spending 52
sport 16–19

studies 32
subjects at school 26–7
suggestions 37
superlatives 77

technology 38–41
tenses
    conditional 104–5
    future 33, 84–5, 98–9
    immediate future 84–5, 98
    imperfect 102–3
    perfect 88–9, 102
    present 81
thé au citron (lemon tea) 12
these / this 51, 75
things to do 56
this / these 51, 75
time 32, 53
to the 36
tous les jours (every day) 13
tout droit (straight on) 55
towns 54–7
transport 59
travel 59
trés (very) 7
tu vas (you go) 59
TV 38–41

uniform, school 29
un peu (a little) 7
un / une changing to de 56

vegetables 12
verbs 78–87
    avoir / être 78–9, 88, 89
    -er / ir / re verbs 80–1, 98
    future plans 31
    holidays 59
    infinitive form 60
    irregular 99, 104
    polite form 14
    reflexive 86–7
    regular 80–1, 104
video games 40–1
vouloir (to want to) 82

weather 61
where I live 4, 8, 54–7
work places 30–1

y (there) 59

Collins

KS3 Revision
French

French

KS3

Workbook

Karine Harrington
Steve Harrison
Sophie Jackson

Contents

KS3 French Workbook

Contents

Family and Home

148 Family
150 House and Home

Lifestyle

152 Food and Drink
154 Sport and Health

Education and Future Plans

156 School and Education
158 Future Plans

Leisure, Free Time and Media

160 Leisure
162 TV and Technology
164 Shopping and Money

The Wider World

166 Where I Live
168 Holidays
170 Global Issues

Grammar

172 Gender and Plurals
173 Adjectives
174 Avoir and Être
175 ER, IR and RE Verbs
176 Modal Verbs
177 Faire, Aller and the Immediate Future
178 Imperative and Reflexive Verbs
179 Perfect Tense
180 Future Tense
181 Pronouns
182 Imperfect Tense
183 Conditional Tense and Passive Voice

184 Mixed Test-Style Questions

205 Answers

216 Revision Tips

Visit our website at **www.collins.co.uk/collinsks3revision** to download the supporting audio material for each topic. This material will provide you with essential practice to improve your listening skills.

Family and Home

Family

1 The box below shows people's birthdays. Match the statements below to the correct person.

Jean 16 / 12 / 99	Amélie 6 / 12 / 97	Alexandre 12 / 4 / 00	Chloé 1 / 1 / 01
Pauline 19 / 7 / 02	Farid 5 / 6 / 95	Karima 15 / 6 / 98	

[5]

a) Mon anniversaire c'est le quinze juin. ....

b) Mon anniversaire c'est le douze avril. ....

c) Mon anniversaire c'est le seize décembre. ....

d) Mon anniversaire c'est le premier janvier. ....

e) Mon anniversaire c'est le dix-neuf juillet. ....

2 Now write out the birthdays of the remaining two people.

a) Mon anniversaire c'est le ....

b) Mon anniversaire c'est le .... [2]

3 Read the descriptions below and then answer the questions that follow.

Myriam Soumaré, athlète:	Ophélie David, skieuse:	Sébastien Chabal, joueur de rugby:	Laure Manaudou, nageuse:
J'ai les cheveux noirs et frisés et j'ai les yeux noirs.	Je suis assez grande. Je mesure 1m72. J'ai les cheveux blonds et les yeux marron.	Je suis très grand et j'ai les cheveux très longs et raides.	J'ai les yeux marron et les cheveux mi-longs.

a) Who has long hair? ....

b) Who is very tall? ....

c) Who has brown eyes? ....

d) Who has black hair? .... [4]

4 Translate the descriptions below into English.

a) J'ai les cheveux bruns, longs et raides. J'ai les yeux bleus et je suis très grande.

.... [6]

b) Je suis assez petit et j'ai les yeux marron. J'ai les cheveux noirs et courts.

_____ **[5]**

c) Nous sommes jumeaux. Nous avons les cheveux blonds, raides et très courts.

_____ **[6]**

d) J'ai un petit chat noir.

_____ **[3]**

5 Read what Marcel, Lucie and Isabelle have to say about themselves, then answer the questions below.

Bonjour! Je m'appelle Marcel et j'habite à la Réunion, c'est une île dans l'océan Pacifique. Je parle français et créole. J'ai une famille nombreuse: j'ai deux sœurs et trois frères et j'habite avec mes parents. Mon anniversaire c'est le treize mai, alors j'ai presque quinze ans.

Bonjour! Je m'appelle Lucie et j'habite au Québec avec ma mère. Mon anniversaire c'est le trente mai. J'ai treize ans. Mes parents sont divorcés. J'ai un demi-frère qui s'appelle Arthur. C'est encore un bébé, il a un an.

Salut! Je m'appelle Isabelle et je suis belge. Je parle français et flamand. J'habite avec mes parents et mes deux frères. Mes frères sont jumeaux et ils ont dix ans. Ma mère s'appelle Christine et elle a quarante ans. Mon père a quarante-cinq ans.

What do the numbers below represent?

Example: 1 is Arthur's age.

a) 13 is _____

b) 14 is _____

c) 40 is _____

d) 45 is _____

e) 10 is _____ **[5]**

Total Marks _____ **/ 36**

Family and Home

House and Home

1 Rearrange the words below to make French sentences and then translate them into English.

a) dans de j'habite la France le nord ....

....

b) maison centre-ville se trouve ma au ....

....

c) dix chez pièces nous il y a...

....

d) de nous avons n' pas jardin ....

....

e) grenier maison et notre deux a étages un ....

....

f) trois étage au premier chambres il y a ....

....

g) de chambre la mes parents est ma de chambre à côté ....

....

h) jolie très petite ma est chambre mais ....

....

i) dans il y a beaucoup choses ma de chambre ....

....

j) dans je télévision n' pas de ai ma chambre ....

....

[10]

2 Insert **mon**, **ma** or **mes** into the sentences below.

a) _____ maison est très grande.

b) Dans _____ chambre j'ai un ordinateur.

c) _____ ordinateur est sur _____ bureau.

d) La chambre de _____ parents est à côté de la chambre

   de _____ frère.

e) _____ ville est dans le sud de la France.

f) _____ cousins habitent au Québec.

g) _____ grand-mère habite avec nous.

h) _____ jardin est petit.   [10]

3 Draw a line to match the questions and answers.

Où habites-tu?	Oui parce que mes amis y habitent aussi.
Tu habites loin de la mer?	Oui, je fais souvent le ménage.
Tu aimes ta ville?	Non, mais nous avons un ordinateur dans le salon.
Comment est ta maison?	Il y a mon lit et mon armoire.
Tu as un jardin?	Elle est assez petite.
Tu aides tes parents à la maison?	Non, assez près, à environ cinq minutes.
Qu'est-ce qu'il y a dans ta chambre?	J'habite en Corse, près de la mer.
Tu as un ordinateur dans ta chambre?	Oui et il est très grand.

[8]

Total Marks _____ / 28

Lifestyle

1 Look at the images below and then make a note of the correct price.

a) **un sandwich au jambon** ....

b) **du poisson** ....

c) **du poulet** ....

d) **des pommes** ....

e) **une bouteille de limonade** ....

f) **un jus d'orange** ....

[6]

2 Read the menu from a French restaurant and choose a dish for the following people.

Sandwich au fromage	Poulet rôti avec des frites
Soupe à l'oignon	Fruits de mer
Omelette aux champignons	Steak-frites
	Tarte à la fraise
Omelette au jambon	Sandwich au thon

a) Paul is a vegetarian but he eats eggs.

....

b) Virginie would like a sandwich but hates fish.

....

c) Olivier has a sweet tooth.

....

d) Laure would like some soup.

_____

e) Philippe likes red meat and chips but doesn't like chicken.

_____ [5]

3 Read the following text and fill in the blanks by choosing a word from the box.

| lait | italienne | orange | spaghettis | pizzas | limonade |

Moi, je préfère la cuisine _____ parce que j'aime les pâtes et les _____

J'adore les _____ à la bolognaise. Comme dessert, j'aime les glaces.

D'habitude, je bois du jus d'_____ parce que je n'aime pas tellement les boissons

gazeuses, comme la _____ Je prends quelquefois une boisson chaude, du café au

_____, par exemple. [6]

4 Read the following statements. What opinion is given about food and drink?

- Write *P* for a *positive* opinion.

- Write *N* for a *negative* opinion.

- Write *P / N* for a *positive* and a *negative* opinion.

a) Je mange des poires parce que j'aime beaucoup le goût. ____

b) Je mange beaucoup de légumes parce que c'est bon pour la santé. ____

c) Je ne mange pas de haricots verts parce que je n'aime pas les légumes. ____

d) J'adore le fromage mais c'est mauvais pour la santé. ____

e) Je bois du thé tous les jours. ____

f) Je ne bois jamais de café. ____

g) Je mange de temps en temps du steak, mais c'est cher. ____

h) Je trouve les biscuits trop sucrés. ____ [8]

Total Marks ____ / 25

Lifestyle

1 Link the following sentences together.

Le weekend, j'aime aller à la piscine,	comme la voile.
Le weekend, j'aime faire de l'équitation.	J'aime les chevaux.
Je fais souvent du vélo.	où je fais de la natation.
J'adore les sports nautiques	J'adore le cyclisme.
J'aime regarder le foot.	mais je tombe souvent.
J'aime le patinage	Je vais souvent au stade.

[6]

2 Read the following information about different sports and decide if the writer has a *positive (P)* attitude, a *negative (N)* attitude or has a *mixed (P / N)* attitude to the sport.

a) Le hockey ne me plaît pas parce que je le trouve très ennuyeux. ....

b) Je vais souvent à la piscine avec mes copains mais c'est assez cher. ....

c) Mon ami adore le ski mais pour moi c'est un sport dangereux. ....

d) J'aime bien le football. Je le trouve marrant et passionnant. ....

e) La gymnastique me fait du bien mais je la trouve fatigante. ....

f) Je trouve le tennis passionnant. Mon joueur favori est Andy Murray. ....

g) En revanche le handball ne m'intéresse pas. C'est très monotone. ....

h) Je recommande les sports d'hiver. L'année dernière j'ai fait du ski dans les

Alpes et c'était fantastique. ....

[8]

3 The people below are describing how they stay healthy. Which picture is relevant to what each is saying?

A   B   C   D

E   F   G

a) Je bois un litre d'eau minérale chaque jour. _____

b) Je suis très sportif, je vais souvent au gymnase. _____

c) Je ne fume jamais. _____

d) Je ne bois jamais de café. _____

e) Je me couche de bonne heure et je dors bien. _____

f) Je ne mange jamais de biscuits ou de gâteaux. _____

g) Je lis un bon livre pour combattre le stress. _____   [7]

4 Fill in the blanks in the sentences below by choosing a word from the box.

mauvais	bon	forme	sportif	légumes
cancer	natation	équitation	violent	

a) Je suis très _____. Je joue au tennis et au foot et je fais de la gymnastique.

b) Je déteste le rugby parce que je le trouve dangereux et _____.

c) Le weekend dernier, je suis allé à la piscine où j'ai fait de la _____.

d) Je ne fume pas parce que c'est _____ pour la santé et ça cause le _____.

e) Pour garder la _____, je mange beaucoup de fruits et de _____.   [7]

Total Marks _____ / 28

Education and Future Plans

School and Education

1 Match the images to the subjects being talked about below.

A   B   C   D

E   F   G

a) Je veux passer le bac, parce que je vais étudier les sciences. _____

b) J'aime beaucoup l'anglais, mais le prof n'est pas sympa. _____

c) J'aime bien le français malgré le professeur. _____

d) Je vais travailler dur, surtout en informatique. _____

e) Je ne peux pas supporter la géographie parce que c'est ennuyeux. _____

f) Je déteste l'histoire. Je suis nul en histoire. _____

[6]

2 Choose the correct word to complete each sentence below.

a) Je n'aime pas l'anglais. Je trouve les cours très _____.

   ennuyeux   intéressants   amusants

b) J'aime aller à l'école parce que j'ai beaucoup _____.

   de copains   de problèmes   de devoirs

c) L'histoire ne me plaît pas. Je la trouve _____.

   trop facile   trop difficile   trop intéressante

d) J'aime mon collège parce que les professeurs sont _____.

   nuls   ennuyeux   sympas

e) Je n'aime pas la chimie parce que je suis _____ en sciences.

   nulle   forte   bien

f) Dans la bibliothèque, il n'y a pas assez de _____.

   frites   chemises   livres

[6]

3 Decide whether these school rules are true or false.

a) **Il ne faut pas manger de chewing-gum en classe.** T / F ☐

b) **Il est interdit de fumer dans les toilettes.** T / F ☐

c) **On ne peut pas jouer au football à la bibliothèque.** T / F ☐

d) **On doit téléphoner à ses amis en classe.** T / F ☐

e) **Il n'est pas permis d'écrire des graffiti aux murs.** T / F ☐

f) **Il est interdit de faire les devoirs.** T / F ☐ **[6]**

4 Read what Claire, Arthur and Salma think about their schools.

Claire

J'aime bien mon école. J'ai beaucoup de copains et on s'amuse bien. Mais la cantine est trop petite et on n'a pas assez d'ordinateurs.

Arthur

Je déteste l'ambiance dans mon collège. C'est très stressant. Pour les profs, seuls les devoirs sont importants. Je ne peux pas sortir en semaine parce j'ai trop de travail scolaire.

Salma

Il est souvent très difficile de bien travailler en classe parce que beaucoup d'élèves sont paresseux et ne font pas attention. Ils ne travaillent pas et ils n'écoutent pas le prof.

Who says the following?

a) I find school very stressful. ⎯⎯⎯⎯⎯⎯⎯⎯⎯⎯

b) I get on with my friends. ⎯⎯⎯⎯⎯⎯⎯⎯⎯⎯

c) Other pupils misbehave. ⎯⎯⎯⎯⎯⎯⎯⎯⎯⎯

d) I would like a larger canteen. ⎯⎯⎯⎯⎯⎯⎯⎯⎯⎯

e) I have so much work I can't go out. ⎯⎯⎯⎯⎯⎯⎯⎯⎯⎯

f) The teachers give too much work to the pupils. ⎯⎯⎯⎯⎯⎯⎯⎯⎯⎯

g) I find a lot of the pupils lazy. ⎯⎯⎯⎯⎯⎯⎯⎯⎯⎯

h) I would like more computers in school. ⎯⎯⎯⎯⎯⎯⎯⎯⎯⎯ **[8]**

Total Marks ⎯⎯⎯⎯⎯ / 26

Education and Future Plans

1 Draw a line to match the French time phrases with their English equivalents.

après	in three years
l'année prochaine	afterwards
puis	first of all
à l'avenir	in the future
d'abord	next year
dans trois ans	then / next

[6]

2 Fill in the table with the feminine versions of these jobs.

Masculine	Feminine
avocat	
coiffeur	
directeur	
infirmier	
traducteur	

[5]

3 Complete the sentences below with the correct infinitive from the box.

habiter	avoir	voyager	continuer	quitter	aller

a) Je vais _____ le collège.

b) Je vais _____ mes études.

c) Je vais _____ à l'université.

d) Je vais _____ à l'étranger.

e) Je vais _____ dans une grande maison.

f) Je vais _____ des enfants.

[6]

4 Rearrange the words in French below so that they make sense. Then translate them into English.

a) dois être je motivé ....

Translation ....

b) faut avec il ses coopérer collègues ....

Translation ....

c) communiquer je mes peux idées ....

Translation .... **[6]**

5 Read what Anna says below and answer the questions in English.

> Je m'appelle Anna et je suis traductrice. J'aime le travail donc je me sens toujours motivé et en plus je peux travailler seule ou en équipe alors c'est très varié. À l'Université, j'ai étudié le français et l'espagnol donc je peux communiquer avec beaucoup de personnes différentes. J'adore mon boulot car c'est intéressant et vraiment bien payé. À l'avenir je veux travailler à l'étranger car ce serait gratifiant et très stimulant.

a) What is Anna's job?

.... **[1]**

b) Why does Anna say her job is varied?

.... **[2]**

c) What has studying French and Spanish allowed her to do?

.... **[1]**

d) Why does she like her job?

.... **[2]**

e) What would she like to do in the future and why?

....

.... **[3]**

Total Marks .... **/ 32**

Leisure, Free Time and Media

Leisure

1 Match the correct time to the sentences below.

| 10:00 | 9:15 | 12:00 | 8:45 |

| 3:30 | 13:30 | 8:00 | 20:00 |

a) Rendez-vous demain à neuf heures et quart. _____

b) Rendez-vous tout à l'heure à midi. _____

c) Rendez-vous mercredi à neuf heures moins le quart. _____

d) Rendez-vous samedi à vingt heures. _____

e) Rendez-vous dimanche à treize heures trente. _____ **[5]**

2 Draw a line to match up two halves to complete a question.

Tu veux aller au		patinoire ce soir?
Tu veux aller à la		à dix heures?
Tu veux		neuf heures demain?
On y va		concert de Stromae avec nous?
On va à la piscine à		venir avec nous au Parc Astérix le weekend prochain?

[5]

3 Complete this note inviting someone to go out.

Tu veux aller *au / à la* (a) _____ **avec moi** (b) _____ (day) **à**

(c) _____ (time)?

Rendez-vous *devant / derrière / dans* (d) _____ (place) **à**

(e) _____ (time). **[5]**

4 Look at the pictures below. Each place has a meeting time. Select **au** or **à la** and insert the correct place and time in the sentences that follow.

a)

b)

c)

d)

e)

a) On va *au/à la* .... à ....

b) On va *au/à la* .... à ....

c) On va *au/à la* .... à ....

d) On va *au/à la* .... à ....

e) On va *au/à la* .... à .... [10]

5 Rearrange the order of the sentences below so that the conversation makes sense.

a) Chouette. À plus!

b) Il y a '*Le Monstre à Paris*' et le film commence à quatorze heures.

c) Ok, à demain!

d) Oui, bonne idée. Qu'est-ce qu'il y a en ce moment?

e) Génial. J'adore les dessins animés. Rendez-vous devant le cinéma à treize heures trente?

f) Non, dans le cinéma car il fait froid.

g) Salut, ça va? Tu veux aller au cinéma demain? [7]

Total Marks .... / 32

Leisure, Free Time and Media

1 Fill in the missing letters in these types of TV programme and state what they are in English.

a) U_ d_s_ _ n _ni_ _ ....

b) _ ne s_ _ _ e ....

c) U _ _ _o_ _ die ....

d) _a m_t_ _ ....

e) L _ _ _n_ _ _ .... **[10]**

2 Draw lines to match the French frequency words with their English equivalents.

de temps en temps	rarely
le weekend	once or twice a week
rarement	often
souvent	from time to time
tous les jours	at the weekend
une / deux fois par semaine	everyday

[6]

3 Read the sentence below.

Je regarde de temps en temps la météo même si c'est assez barbant.

a) Which word is a connective? ....

b) Which word is a frequency word? ....

c) Which word is an intensifier? .... **[3]**

4 Add a frequency word, a connective, an intensifier and an opinion to the following sentence:

Je regarde les émissions de sport.

....

.... **[4]**

5 Read what Madeleine says below and answer the questions in English.

> Je m'appelle Madeleine et j'adore regarder la télé, pourtant ma mère n'aime pas ça donc je ne la regarde que deux fois par semaine. Normalement je regarde les émissions de télé-réalité car elles sont vraiment marrantes mais mon frère aime les séries donc parfois nous regardons les séries policières.

a) What is Madeleine's mother's opinion of TV?

_____ [1]

b) How often does Madeleine watch TV?

_____ [1]

c) Why does she watch reality TV shows?

_____ [1]

d) With whom does she like to watch police series and how often?

_____ [2]

6 You have been asked to write an article in French for the school magazine about the advantages of modern technology. List five possible advantages in French.

_____

_____

_____

_____

_____

_____

_____

_____

_____

[5]

Total Marks _____ / 33

Leisure, Free Time and Media

Shopping and Money

1 How much pocket money does this person receive?

Je reçois vingt euros par mois. .... **[2]**

2 Translate each of these clothing materials into English.

a) **en coton** ....

b) **en cuir** ....

c) **en laine** .... **[3]**

3 Each phrase below contains a mistake. Rewrite them so that they are correct.

a) **une bleue jupe** ....

b) **un pantalon grise** ....

c) **une cravate jaunee** ....

d) **un noir pull** ....

e) **une chemise violet** ....

f) **des chaussures marrons** .... **[6]**

4 Write the French word for each item of clothing below.

a)

b)

....

c)

d)

....   **[4]**

5 Read what Céline says and answer the questions below in English.

> Je m'appelle Céline et mon père me donne quarante euros par mois – c'est vraiment généreux! Avec mon argent de poche j'achète des CDs et du maquillage mais j'essaie aussi de faire des économies pour acheter un nouveau vélo.

a) Who gives Celine her pocket money?

_____ [1]

b) How much does she receive?

_____ [2]

c) What does she buy with her money?

_____ [2]

d) What else does she do with her money and why?

_____ [2]

6 Read what Chloé, Paul and Ann-Lou say below about their pocket money.

Chloé: Ma grand-mère me donne dix euros par semaine.

Paul: Je reçois trente euros par mois.

Ann-Lou: Mes parents me donnent un euro par jour.

Who receives the most pocket money? _____ [1]

7 Translate the sentence below into French.

I receive 20 euros per week because I look after my little brother. With my pocket money I buy clothes and I save.

_____

_____ [4]

Total Marks _____ / 27

The Wider World

Where I Live

1 The places in the box are described in the sentences below. Match the correct place to each sentence.

l'hôtel de ville	une banque	le centre de recyclage
un jardin public	la gare	le centre de loisirs
un centre commercial		

a) C'est un endroit où l'on peut recycler le verre, le papier etc. ....

b) On y trouve des trains. ....

c) C'est l'endroit où tout le monde peut faire du shopping. ....

d) On peut y changer de l'argent. ....

e) C'est un endroit où il y a des arbres et des fleurs. ....

f) On peut y faire du sport. ....   [6]

2 Follow the directions below and chose the letter that shows your destination. Each time your starting point is at the bottom.

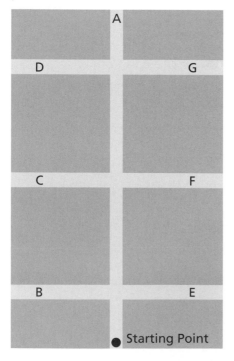

a) Pour aller au cinéma, continuez tout droit. ....

b) Pour aller au marché, prenez la deuxième rue à gauche. ....

c) **Pour aller à la poste, prenez la troisième rue à droite.** ....

d) **Pour aller au parc, prenez la deuxième rue à droite.** ....

e) **L'hôtel de ville? Prenez la première rue à gauche.** .... **[5]**

3 Read about these excursions in the town. Note down in English where each excursion goes, what you can do and how you get there.

a) **Visite de la vieille ville. Promenade pour voir les églises. Visite à pied.**

....

....

b) **Excursion au jardin public, pour voir les roses. Départ du bus à dix heures.**

....

.... **[6]**

4 Read Aurélie's description of her town and answer the questions in English.

Rouen se trouve dans le nord-ouest de la France. C'est une grande ville industrielle. Il y a un centre commercial, un centre sportif, une piscine, un stade, un théâtre, un cinéma et une bibliothèque.

J'aime bien habiter ici parce qu'il y a beaucoup à faire et c'est très animé. Il y a aussi beaucoup de touristes. Il y a la cathédrale, des musées et la vieille ville.

Je n'aime pas la campagne. Je préfère la ville parce que la campagne est trop calme, il n'y a rien à faire. Les transports en commun ne sont pas fréquents.

a) Where in France is Rouen? ....

b) Name two buildings you can see there. ....

c) Why does Patricia like living there? ....

d) Name two things which tourists can visit. ....

e) What does she think of the countryside and why? Give two reasons. ....

.... **[8]**

Total Marks .... **/ 25**

The Wider World

Holidays

1 Match the French time phrases with the English equivalents.

une semaine et demie	a fortnight
deux semaines	ten days
quinze jours	one month
un mois	two weeks
dix jours	one and a half weeks

[5]

2 Fill the gaps in the sentences below to describe what each person does for their holidays.
The English is given in brackets but you need to write the French and also circle **en**, **au** or **à** for each place.

a) **Normalement je vais** *en/au/à* (Paris) _____ **avec** (family)
_____ **pour** (one week) _____

b) **Normalement je vais** *en/au/à* (Canada) _____ **avec** (parents)
_____ **pour** (one month) _____

c) **Normalement je vais** *en/au/à* (Lyon) _____ **avec** (grandparents)
_____ **pour** (two weeks) _____

d) **Normalement je vais** *en/au/à* (England) _____ **avec** (my mum)
_____ **pour** (ten days) _____

e) **Normalement je vais** *en/au/à* (Spain) _____ **avec** (my dad)
_____ **pour** (one week) _____

[15]

3 Match the pictures to the descriptions of people's holidays below.

A  B  C  D

a) **Salut! Je suis en vacances à Nice et il fait très chaud. Comme le temps est génial je vais à la plage tous les jours et je me fais bronzer!** _____

b) **Bonjour! Je suis en vacances à Montréal, au Canada, et en ce moment c'est l'hiver. Il fait très froid et il neige de temps en temps. Alors je fais beaucoup de courses dans les grands centres commerciaux. J'ai acheté des cadeaux pour tout le monde!** _____

c) **Salut! Je passe mes vacances en Guyane et en ce moment il pleut beaucoup mais il ne fait pas froid. Avec mon parapluie et mes bottes je visite beaucoup de monuments et je prends beaucoup de photos!** _____

d) **Bonjour! Je passe de super vacances ici à Papeete, en Polynésie mais malheureusement il y a eu une tempête récemment et il y a beaucoup de vent tous les jours. Il y a du soleil alors je me promène beaucoup avec ma famille.** _____   **[4]**

4 Translate into French.

a) I would like a room for two nights. _____

b) I would like a room with two beds. _____

c) Do you have a room with a balcony? _____

d) Is there a restaurant? _____

e) Is there a lift in the hotel? _____

f) Is there a swimming pool? _____

g) My room is dirty. _____

h) The television is not working. _____

i) The shower is broken. _____   **[9]**

The Wider World

Global Issues

1 Match up the global issues in French to the correct term in English.

le changement climatique	deforestation
la déforestation	recycling
l'énergie nucléaire	oil slicks
les inondations	climate change
les marées noires	over-fishing
le recyclage	floods
la surpêche	nuclear energy

[7]

2 a) Translate **il faut** into English.

.... [1]

b) What kind of verb must follow **il faut**?

.... [1]

3 Give the meanings of the following imperatives.

a) Jetez! ....

b) Évitez! ....

c) Réduisez! ....

d) Soutenez! ....

e) Sauvez! .... [5]

4 Use two of the imperatives in question 3 to form appropriate commands.

e.g. Évitez la déforestation!

.... [1]

.... [1]

5 What are the concerns of the four people below and what are they doing to help solve the problem?

Answer in English.

a)
> **Ce qui me préoccupe le plus c'est la pauvreté donc je donne aux organisations de bienfaisance.**

Concern: ....

Solution: ....

....

b)
> **Je suis contre la déforestation – c'est un vrai problème donc à mon avis il faut recycler le papier.**

Concern: ....

Solution: ....

....

c)
> **Moi, j'essaie d'organiser des événements pour combattre la faim. C'est le problème le plus grave.**

Concern: ....

Solution: ....

....

d)
> **Je m'inquiète sur les espèces menacées et je crois qu'il est nécessaire de protéger les animaux.**

Concern: ....

Solution: ....

.... **[8]**

6 Using question 5 to help you, write in French one of your concerns and give a possible solution.

....

....

....

....

.... **[2]**

Total Marks .... **/ 26**

Grammar

Gender and Plurals

1 Are these words masculine or feminine? Write **un** or **une** for each one.

a) .... souris   f) .... appartement

b) .... table   g) .... famille

c) .... fille   h) .... chien

d) .... père   i) .... cousin

e) .... chat   j) .... cousine   [10]

2 Write these words in the plural form.

a) un bateau ....   f) un journal ....

b) un tapis ....   g) une table ....

c) un chapeau ....   h) un nez ....

d) un cheval ....   i) un château ....

e) une souris ....   j) un animal ....   [10]

3 Fill in the gaps in this text about theme parks in France with appropriate articles. Remember to think about genders and plurals.

Le Futuroscope c'est (a) .... **parc d'attractions dans**

(b) .... **sud ouest de** (c) .... **France. Il y a**

(d) .... **cinémas intéractifs et beaucoup** (e) ....

spectacles incroyables.

Le parc Astérix c'est comme (f) .... **village gaulois avec Astérix et**

Obélix, qui sont .... (g) **personnages de bandes dessinées. Astérix a**

(h) .... **cheveux blonds et** (i) .... **gros nez. Obélix a**

(j) .... **gros ventre et** (k) .... **cheveux roux. Ils ont**

(l) .... **petit chien blanc, qui s'appelle Idéfix.**   [12]

Total Marks .... / 32

Adjectives

1 Circle all the adjectives in the box below.

petit	sœur	grand	rouge	aller	sympa
la France	manger	paresseux	maison	français	Paris

[6]

2 Complete each sentence by adding an opposite adjective from the list below. Remember to add the correct ending of each adjective.

ancien	gros	hivernal	dégoûtant	grand

a) La Corse est petite mais la France est ....

b) Astérix est mince mais Obélix est ....

c) Moi, je pense que la quiche lorraine est bonne mais les escargots sont ....

d) Le Centre Pompidou est moderne mais le Louvre est ....

e) La fête de la Musique le 21 juin est une fête estivale mais l'Épiphanie, le 6 janvier, est

une fête ....

[5]

3 Fill each gap below using an adjective in French with the correct ending. The English is given in brackets.

Salut! Je m'appelle Lisa et j'ai deux (a) .... (little) **sœurs. Céline est très**

(b) .... (tall) **et elle a les cheveux** (c) .... (black),

mais Sophie est (d) .... (blond), **comme moi. Nous sommes très**

(e) .... (sporty) **mais quelquefois un peu** (f) .... (lazy).

J'ai aussi un demi-frère qui est (g) .... (older than) **nous. Céline est la**

(h) .... (tallest) **et Sophie est la** (i) .... (smallest). **Je**

suis (j) .... (the best). [10]

Total Marks .... / 21

Grammar

Avoir and Être

1 Match up each subject with the correct form of **être** to complete each sentence.

Je	est la capitale de la France.
Paris	sont des athlètes.
Aurélie Joly et Myriam Soumaré	sommes originaires de la Guadeloupe.
Tu	suis français.
Nous	es parisien?

[5]

2 Fill in the gaps with the appropriate forms of **être** and **avoir**.

a) J'habite en Guyane et je _____ française. En Guyane nous _____ une forêt équatoriale et plein de tortues! Il y _____ beaucoup de soleil.

b) Tu _____ française ou pas? Le français _____ la langue officielle au Québec?

c) Mes cousins habitent en Guadeloupe, ils _____ français.

d) Nous habitons maintenant à Marseille qui _____ dans le sud de la France mais nous _____ originaires de Bordeaux dans le sud-ouest. J' _____ aussi beaucoup de cousins dans les Alpes.

e) La Réunion _____ une île à l'est de Madagascar et il y _____ un volcan.

f) Lyon _____ la deuxième grande ville de France. [12]

3 Translate each of these sentences into French with the correct use of **avoir**.

a) I am 14 and my sister is 16. _____

b) How old is your sister? _____

c) My friend is the same age as me. _____

d) Are you thirsty? _____

e) I am very hungry _____ [5]

Total Marks _____ / 22

ER, IR and RE Verbs

1 Match up each English verb with its French equivalent.

to eat	finir
to sing	vendre
to like	choisir
to live	manger
to finish	chanter
to choose	habiter
to wait	aimer
to sell	attendre

[8]

2 What endings would you add to the stem of the verbs? Fill in the table with the appropriate endings.

	je	tu	il / elle	nous	vous	ils / elles
-ER verbs	-e					-ent
-IR verbs		-is				
-RE verbs	-s		nothing		-ez	

[12]

3 Choose the correct verb form in brackets to complete each sentence.

a) En France, le 14 juillet, on _____ (fête / fêtent / fêtons) la fête nationale.

b) J' _____ (aimes / aime / aiment) chanter la Marseillaise, notre hymne national.

c) Nous sommes français et nous _____ (habite / habitent / habitons) en Guadeloupe.

d) En Guadeloupe, pendant le carnaval, nous _____ (danse / dansons / dansez) beaucoup.

e) En France, l'école _____ (finissont / finit / finis) normalement vers seize heures trente ou dix-sept heures.

f) À Noël, les petits enfants _____ (attendons / attendent / attends) le père Noël avec impatience!

g) Bonjour madame, vous _____ (vendent / vendez / vends) du pain ici? [7]

Total Marks _____ / 27

Grammar

Modal Verbs

1 Choose the correct form of the verb in each sentence below. Then translate each sentence into English.

a) Je *veux / veut / veulent* aller en ville.

_____

b) Ils *dois / doit / doivent* acheter des cadeaux.

_____

c) Nous ne *pouvoir / pouvons / pouvez* pas aller au cinéma.

_____

d) Fatima *dois / doit / devoir* faire ses devoirs de maths.

_____

e) Vous *vouloir / voulons / voulez* venir avec nous?

_____ **[10]**

2 Fill in the gaps with the correct form of the verb in brackets.

a) Je _____ (vouloir) faire du vélo.

b) Tu _____ (pouvoir) venir chez moi ce soir?

c) Elle _____ (devoir) faire ses devoirs.

d) Je ne _____ (pouvoir) pas sortir samedi soir.

e) Elles _____ (vouloir) acheter des cadeaux de Noël.

f) Nous _____ (devoir) travailler dur.

g) Vous _____ (pouvoir) m'aider? **[7]**

3 Using the modal verbs above, translate the following sentences into French.

a) Can you come to my house? _____

b) I want to go out on Saturday evening. _____

c) She must work hard. _____

d) The friends can go cycling. _____

e) We want to buy some presents. _____ **[5]**

Total Marks _____ / 22

Faire, Aller and the Immediate Future

1 Write out these sentences in the immediate future, using the correct form of the verb **aller** and the infinitive.

Example: **Je mange au restaurant.**

  Je vais manger au restaurant.

a) **Mon frère regarde la télé.** ....

b) **Les deux filles dansent.** ....

c) **Tu écoutes de la musique?** ....

d) **Je joue au foot dans le jardin.** ....

e) **Nous sortons ensemble.** .... **[5]**

2 Put these sentences into the plural, changing **je** to **nous, tu** to **vous** and **il / elle** to **ils / elles**.

a) **Je fais du ski en hiver.** ....

b) **Tu fais souvent du vélo?** ....

c) **Il fait un gros gâteau au chocolat.** ....

d) **Elle fait une promenade à la campagne.** .... **[4]**

3 Fill in the correct form of the verb **aller** in the following sentences.

Here are all six possible forms: **vais, vas, va, allons, allez, vont.**

a) **Les filles** .... **au théâtre.**

b) **Samedi, nous** .... **au parc d'attractions.**

c) **Je ne** .... **jamais au marché.**

d) **Est-ce que vous y** .... **avec votre frère?**

e) **Tu** .... **aux magasins?**

f) **Grégoire** .... **au stade.** **[6]**

Total Marks .... **/ 15**

Grammar

Imperative and Reflexive Verbs

1 Translate these imperative phrases into English.

a) **Fermez la porte!** ....

b) **Mangeons maintenant.** ....

c) **Ne parle pas!** ....

d) **Joue avec ta sœur!** ....

e) **Allez chez le dentiste!** ....

f) **Écoutons de la musique!** ....

g) **N'entrez pas dans le salon!** ....

h) **Sortez immédiatement!** .... [8]

2 Fill in the gaps in the sentences below with the correct form of the verb chosen from the box.

me lève	se lève	se lèvent	te couches	vous couchez
me lave	nous lavons	s'habillent	s'habille	

a) **Les enfants** .... **quand le professeur entre dans la salle de classe.**

b) **À quelle heure est-ce que tu** .... **?**

c) **Tous les jours, nous** .... **dans la salle de bains.**

d) **Juliette** .... **dans sa chambre. Elle met une jupe, un pull et un chemisier.**

e) **Avant de manger, je** .... **les mains.** [5]

3 Translate the following sentences about daily routine into French.

a) I wake up at seven o'clock. ....

b) He gets up at quarter past seven. ....

c) You have a wash in the bathroom. ....

d) She gets dressed in her bedroom. ....

e) They relax in the living room. ....

f) I go to bed at ten o'clock. .... [6]

Total Marks .... **/ 19**

Perfect Tense

1 Translate these perfect tense sentences into English.

a) J'ai fait du shopping samedi après-midi. _____

b) Nous avons regardé un DVD ensemble. _____

c) Tu as vu le film? _____

d) Je suis sortie avec mes copines. _____

e) Elle est restée à la maison. _____

f) Il a répondu à ma question. _____

g) Vous avez choisi un livre? _____ [7]

2 Change these sentences into the perfect tense.

a) Je mange un sandwich au fromage. _____

b) Julie joue de la guitare. _____

c) Nous écoutons de la musique. _____

d) Tu finis tes devoirs? _____

e) Vous nagez dans la mer? _____

f) Elle va au supermarché. _____

g) Les deux amis arrivent à deux heures. _____

h) Je fais du ski nautique. _____ [8]

3 Translate these perfect tense sentences into French.

a) I went to the park. _____

b) We saw the film. _____

c) He did not eat the cake. _____

d) She entered the house. _____

e) You spoke to his father. _____

f) The three girls stayed in the classroom. _____

g) I have bought some shoes. _____

h) He has arrived at the station. _____ [8]

Total Marks _____ / 23

Grammar

Future Tense

1 Circle the odd one out in each row.

a) jouerai   jouaient   jouerez   jouera

b) mangeons   mangerons   mangeront   mangeras

c) irez   iront   ira   irait

d) vendons   vendez   vendent   vendrez   **[4]**

2 Complete the following future tense table.

Infinitive	Stem	Future tense
visiter	visiter	il visitera
écouter		tu
choisir		je
perdre		ils
être		nous
avoir		vous

[10]

3 Correct the error in each of these future tense sentences.

a) **Je mangeras une pomme.**

_____

b) **Nous attendons le bus.**

_____

c) **Elle irai au cinéma.**

_____

d) **Ils visitèrent le musée.**

_____ **[4]**

Pronouns

1 Name the types of pronouns used in each of the phrases below.

a) **Elle, elle adore le tennis** _____

b) **Nous l'aimons beaucoup** _____

c) **Vous êtes vraiment belle** _____

d) **Il leur téléphone** _____ **[4]**

2 Decide whether to use **y** or **en** in each of these phrases.

a) **On** _____ **va. (On va à la piscine.)**

b) **Tu** _____ **veux? (Tu veux des chips?)**

c) **Il** _____ **voudrait. (Il voudrait de la pizza.)**

d) **Nous** _____ **passons toujours le weekend. (Nous passons toujours le weekend chez notre père.)** **[4]**

3 Rewrite the following sentences using a subject pronoun and a direct object pronoun where appropriate.

a) **Le père adore ses filles.** _____

b) **Les enfants chantent la chanson.** _____

c) **Sandra regarde le match de tennis.** _____ **[6]**

4 Fill in the missing reflexive pronoun in each of the phrases below.

a) **Elles** _____ **lavent.**

b) **Tu** _____ **réveilles.**

c) **Je** _____ **habille.**

d) **On** _____ **couche.**

e) **Nous** _____ **levons.** **[5]**

Total Marks _____ / 19

Grammar

Imperfect Tense

1 Explain when you would use the perfect and the imperfect tense to talk about an action in the past.

Perfect tense: .... **[1]**

....

Imperfect tense: ....

.... **[3]**

2 Complete the following imperfect tense table.

Infinitive	Stem	Imperfect tense
finir	finiss	je finissais
aller		tu
vendre		il
dormir		nous
perdre		vous
parler		elles

[10]

3 Translate the imperfect tense sentences below into French.

a) I used to play football.

....

b) He visited the exhibition every day.

....

c) We used to go to the park at the weekend.

....

d) You (polite) used to be funny.

.... **[4]**

Total Marks .... **/ 18**

Conditional Tense and Passive Voice

1 Circle the conditional tense in each of the following sentences.

a) J'irais au cinéma si j'aimais les films d'action.

b) Si je n'étais pas végétarien, je mangerais de la viande.

c) Elle achèterait la robe si elle avait plus d'argent de poche. [3]

2 Write whether each of the sentences below is an example of the passive or the active voice.

a) Sara regarde le film. _____

b) Le livre est détesté par Will. _____

c) La souris est mangée par le chat. _____

d) Violette a trouvé ses clés. _____ [4]

3 Change the following active voice sentences into the passive voice. Watch your tenses!

a) Luc achète le magazine.

_____

b) Zara a mangé de la soupe.

_____

c) Thomas dessinera le mannequin.

_____

d) La chorale chante les chansons.

_____ [4]

4 Translate the passive voice sentences below into English.

a) Elle a été vue.

_____

b) Il est aimé de tout le monde.

_____

c) Il sera puni.

_____ [6]

Total Marks _____ / 17

Mixed Test-Style Questions

1 Match up the sentences to the correct time.

Il est huit heures trente.	00:00
Il est dix-neuf heures.	14:15
Il est sept heures.	1:45
Il est deux heures moins le quart.	19:00
Il est minuit.	8:30
Il est quatorze heures quinze.	7:00

6 marks

2 Read the weather forecast below and then choose a symbol for each town.

La météo pour aujourd'hui.

Aujourd'hui il fait très beau dans toute la France. Il y a du soleil à Paris et il fait très chaud à Marseille, environ 30 degrés. Mais attention au brouillard ce matin dans le nord et surtout à Lille et les nuages arrivent dans l'ouest. Il y a donc du vent près des côtes et particulièrement à Brest.

A)   B)    C)    D)

a) Paris ....

b) Marseille ....

c) Lille ....

d) Brest ....

4 marks

3 Read the opinions about festivities in France and answer the questions that follow.

Léa

Moi j'adore le 14 juillet, notre fête nationale, car il y a beaucoup de feux d'artifice* et il y a un bal dans mon village. Tout le monde danse et chante jusqu' à très tard et je trouve ça chouette.

*fireworks

Enzo

Moi je préfère Noël bien sûr! Le 24 décembre au soir je mange un grand repas avec toute ma famille et le 25 décembre j'ouvre tous mes cadeaux. Comme j'habite dans les Alpes il neige souvent à Noël.

Lola

Ma fête préférée c'est l'Épiphanie, le 6 janvier. Ce jour-là on mange une galette qui s'appelle la *galette des Rois*. Dans la galette il y a un petit objet qui s'appelle *la fève***. La personne qui a la fève est le roi ou la reine et porte une couronne!

*a puff pastry pie filled with frangipane
**a little figurine hidden in the pie

Olivier

J'aime beaucoup Pâques! J'adore chercher mes œufs en chocolat dans le jardin. C'est très amusant.

Questions:

a) Who likes Easter? _____

b) Who likes Christmas? _____

c) When is the French national day celebrated? _____

d) On what day do they eat **la galette des Rois** in France? _____

e) Who becomes a queen or a king on that day? _____

f) What does Olivier hunt for in his garden? _____

6 marks

TOTAL

16

4 Write down in English what pets each of these people has.

a) J'ai un chien et deux chats.

....

b) J'ai un petit chien blanc.

....

c) J'ai trois poissons rouges.

....

d) J'ai deux chevaux.

....

e) Je n'ai pas d'animaux.

....

5 marks

5 A class of 30 pupils were asked what their favourite and least favourite colours are. Read the results below and then answer the questions that follow.

Quelle est ta couleur préférée?	**Quelle est la couleur que tu n'aimes pas?**
Quinze élèves ont dit: le bleu	Dix élèves ont dit: le jaune
Dix élèves ont dit: le violet	Sept élèves ont dit: le marron
Cinq élèves ont dit: le rose	Sept élèves ont dit: le rose
	Six élèves ont dit: le vert

a) What is the most popular colour? ....

b) How many pupils do not like green? ....

c) How many pupils said they did not like brown? ....

d) How many pupils mentioned pink? ....

e) What colour has been mentioned the most? ....

f) What colour has been mentioned the least? ....

6 marks

6 Read what Maëva says about her holiday and then answer the questions in English.

> D'habitude je vais en vacances en Guadeloupe car toute ma famille y habite. On parle français et créole en Guadeloupe. J'y vais avec ma mère, mon beau-père et mon demi-frère. On y va normalement pour trois semaines au mois d'août et on loge dans un hôtel. Comme il fait toujours beau et chaud, on va tous les jours à la plage. J'adore aller en Guadeloupe parce qu'il y a un super caranaval chaque été et la nourriture est très bonne.

a) Where does she normally go?

_____

b) Why does she go there?

_____

c) What languages do they speak there?

_____

d) Who exactly does she go with?

_____

e) When do they usually go?

_____

f) How long do they go for?

_____

g) Where do they stay?

_____

h) What do they do every day?

_____

i) How often does the carnival take place?

_____

j) Apart from the carnival, what does she like about Guadeloupe?

_____

10 marks

TOTAL

21

Mixed Test-Style Questions

7 Imagine you are each of the people below. Write who you are and describe yourself in French.

a) Sébastien: tall, blue eyes and blond hair.

_____

_____

b) Karima: small, brown eyes and long hair.

_____

_____

8 marks

8 Below is an interview with a French football player called Pierre. Fill in the gaps with the appropriate questions from the box below.

Quelle est la date de ton anniversaire?	**Tu parles créole?**
Tu as quel âge?	**Où habites-tu?**
Ça va?	**Tu as des frères et sœurs?**

Reporter: **Bonjour, Pierre.** _____

Pierre: **Oui, très bien, merci.**

Reporter: _____

Pierre: **Je suis né le 20 mars.**

Reporter: _____

Pierre: **C'est un secret!**

Reporter: _____

Pierre: **Oui, un frère et une sœur.**

Reporter: _____

Pierre: **J'habite en France mais mes parents viennent de la Martinique.**

Reporter: _____

Pierre: **Non, malheureusement!**

Reporter: **Merci, Pierre.**

Pierre: **De rien!**

6 marks

9 When is each person's birthday? Write down the date as a number.

a) **Mon anniversaire c'est le trente septembre.** _____

b) **Mon anniversaire c'est le deux mai.** _____

c) **Mon anniversaire c'est le premier août.** _____

d) **Mon anniversaire c'est le treize mars.** _____

e) **Mon anniversaire c'est le douze janvier.** _____

5 marks

10 Read the conversation below between Frédéric and Benjamin and answer the questions in English.

> **Salut! Ça va? Tu veux aller à la patinoire demain?**

> **Bonne idée! C'est à quelle heure?**

> **La séance commence à quatorze heures.**

> **Oh non! Je dois rester chez moi avec ma sœur parce que ma mère travaille et elle finit à quatorze heures.**

> **Pas de problème! Il y a une autre séance plus tard à seize heures.**

> **Génial. On y va à pied? Rendez-vous chez moi à quinze heures?**

> **OK. À demain!**

a) Where are Frédéric and Benjamin planning to go? _____

b) When does Benjamin's friend want to go (time and day)? _____

c) Why can't Benjamin go then? _____

d) How are they planning to get there? _____

e) What solution do they agree on? _____

f) Where and at what time are they meeting up? _____

7 marks

TOTAL

26

Mixed Test-Style Questions

11 Match up the French and English equivalents of these greetings.

Salut!	Hello!
Bonsoir!	Hi!
À bientôt!	Have a good day!
Bon anniversaire!	See you soon!
Bonjour!	Goodbye!
Bonne nuit!	Happy birthday!
Bonne journée!	Good night!
Au revoir!	Good evening!

8 marks

12 The questions below are being asked in a hotel. What is each person asking?

a) **Où est la piscine?** _____

b) **Où est le restaurant?** _____

c) **Il y a un ascenseur?** _____

d) **Il y a une douche dans la chambre?** _____

4 marks

13 Read what the people say about music below and then answer the questions that follow.

Marcel: **Je joue du piano depuis trois ans.**

Lucie: **Je ne joue pas du piano mais je joue de la batterie.**

Sébastien: **Je joue de la guitare.**

Laure: **La guitare c'est ennuyeux. Je préfère jouer du piano.**

Isabelle: **Le violon c'est génial.**

Myriam: **Je joue du violon depuis deux ans mais c'est nul.**

a) Who thinks violin is great? ....

b) Who plays the drums? ....

c) Who doesn't like playing the guitar? ....

d) Who likes playing the piano? ....

4 marks

14 Read the review of the book **Les Malheurs de Sophie** and answer the questions in English that follow.

Les Malheurs de Sophie

Les Malheurs de Sophie est un livre pour enfants écrit par La Comtesse de Ségur.

C'est l'histoire de Sophie, une petite fille qui habite avec ses parents dans un château dans la campagne française. Sophie est très curieuse et aventureuse. Ses copines s'appellent Camille et Madeleine et elles sont très gentilles. Sophie, elle, est souvent méchante et capricieuse et fait beaucoup de bêtises avec son cousin Paul, mais Sophie est très amusante!

a) Who is the book written for?

....

b) Who is the story about?

....

c) Where does the main character live?

....

d) Who are Camille and Madeleine?

....

e) Give one positive adjective that describes the main character?

....

f) Give one negative adjective that describes the main character?

....

7 marks

g) Who is she mischievous with?

....

TOTAL

23

15 Match up the French and English equivalents in these clothing descriptions.

à la mode	stripy
à pois	old-fashioned
cool	ugly
démodé(e)	cool
écossaise(e)	fashionable / trendy
moche	polka dotted
rayé	tartan

7 marks

16 Fill in the gaps in these sentences about television using the words provided.

mais	regarder	fois	jamais	car	vraiment	émouvants

a) Je regarde des feuilletons une _____ par semaine.

b) Je regarde des comédies _____ parfois elles sont

_____ ennuyeuses.

c) J'aime _____ la météo.

d) J'adore regarder des films _____ ils sont très _____.

e) Je ne regarde _____ les infos.

7 marks

17 Choose the correct sport to go with each definition.

le ski	le football	le rugby	le tennis	la natation

a) On va à la piscine pour pratiquer ce sport. _____

b) Il faut une raquette et une balle pour y jouer. _____

c) C'est un sport d'hiver. _____

d) Il y a onze joueurs dans une équipe. _____

e) Il y a quinze joueurs dans une équipe. _____

5 marks

18 Read the following passage in which Salma writes about health issues. Answer the questions in English.

> Il est important de faire du sport. Le sport est relaxant et c'est bon pour le cœur. On se fait aussi de nouveaux amis surtout si on joue en équipe. Je joue souvent au handball avec mes amis. Je vais à la piscine une fois par semaine. Je ne fume pas parce que ça cause le cancer et le tabagisme passif est dangereux pour les autres. Pour me relaxer, je lis un bon livre ou j'écoute de la musique. Je n'ai pas l'intention de boire trop de boissons gazeuses parce que c'est mauvais pour la santé.

a) Why does Salma say sport is important? Give three reasons.

_____

b) Apart from handball, what other sport does she do?

_____

c) Why does she not smoke? Give two reasons.

_____

d) What two things does she do to relax?

_____

e) What is she not going to do in the future, and why?

_____

10 marks

19 Match the French and English equivalents of these opinion phrases.

à mon avis	I believe that
en ce qui me concerne	I think that
je pense que	as far as I am concerned
je crois que	in my opinion

4 marks

TOTAL

33

Mixed Test-Style Questions

20 What do you do with your pocket money? Write at least two things in French.

4 marks

21 Fill in the gaps in the sentences below choosing an appropriate word from the box.

| les pommes   les haricots verts   le poulet   les fromages   du chocolat   la soupe |

a) Je n'aime pas les légumes, par exemple

b) J'adore les fruits, surtout

c) J'aime les choses sucrées et je mange souvent

d) Quand il fait froid, j'aime manger de _____ de légumes.

e) J'aime beaucoup _____ comme le camembert ou le brie.

5 marks

22 Translate the following sentences into French.

a) I don't like music because the teacher is strict.

b) My favourite subject is art because it is easy.

c) I hate science, especially physics.

d) Lessons start at half past eight.

e) At lunchtime, I eat in the canteen with my friends.

f) I go to school by car.

g) Lessons finish at half past three.

h) It is forbidden to talk in class.

8 marks

23 Annie is talking about whether school uniform should be introduced in France. Decide if the statements that follow are true or false.

> Beaucoup de mes amies ne sont pas du tout favorables à l'introduction d'un uniforme scolaire mais je crois que l'uniforme est une très bonne idée parce qu'on ne remarque plus les différences entre les riches et les pauvres. Il y a un garçon dans ma classe qui arrive souvent à l'école avec de nouveaux vêtements très chers. L'uniforme scolaire est aussi très pratique parce que, le matin, on sait ce qu'on va porter. Cependant, je n'aime pas l'idée de porter une cravate. De plus en Angleterre, les filles doivent porter une jupe mais moi, j'aime mieux porter un pantalon.

a) Many of Annie's friends are in favour of having a uniform.   T / F ☐

b) Annie is in favour of school uniform.   T / F ☐

c) There is a girl in her class who wears expensive clothes at school.   T / F ☐

d) Annie thinks a uniform makes it easier to decide what to wear.   T / F ☐

e) She likes the idea of wearing a tie.   T / F ☐

f) She prefers wearing a skirt rather than trousers.   T / F ☐

☐
6 marks

24 Complete the following sentences about a town by choosing a word from the box.

le centre commercial	le musée	la piscine
le stade	le jardin public	la gare

a) Pour ceux qui aiment le shopping, il y a ....

b) Pour ceux qui s'intéressent à l'histoire, il y a ....

c) Pour ceux qui veulent voir un match de foot, il y a ....

d) Pour ceux qui veulent faire de la natation, il y a ....

e) Pour ceux qui aiment faire des promenades dans la nature, il y a ....

☐
5 marks

TOTAL
☐
28

Mixed Test-Style Questions

25 Read these statements about mobile phones and technology. Mark each one A if it is an advantage or D if it is a disadvantage.

a) On peut se tenir au courant. ☐

b) Il y a trop de tyrans sur internet. ☐

c) Il y a des gens qui veulent faire mal aux autres. ☐

d) Ça m'aide à communiquer avec mes amis. ☐

e) Je suis trop préoccupé. ☐

f) Je dépense trop d'argent chaque mois. ☐

g) Il est plus facile de changer des projets. ☐

h) On peut communiquer plus facilement. ☐

i) Je me sens plus en sécurité. ☐

j) C'est mauvais pour la santé. ☐

☐
10 marks

26 Describe your school uniform, mentioning at least three items with three descriptions.

Au collège, je porte... _____

_____

_____

☐
6 marks

27 Read what Guillaume's concerns are below and answer the questions that follow.

> Je m'appelle Guillaume et je m'inquiète pour la planète. Mes priorités sont les animaux et je trouve qu'il y a un grand problème avec la surpêche, la cruauté envers les animaux, et la déforestation qui détruit des habitats. À mon avis il faut faire plus pour protéger les animaux. C'est essentiel pour le futur de la planète!

a) What is Guillaume worried about?

_____

b) What are the big problems affecting animals?

_____

c) What is the consequence of deforestation?

....

d) What must be done?

....

28 Circle the correct answer for each description of food and drink below.

a) C'est un fruit rouge.

    une banane   **une fraise**   **un citron**

b) C'est un légume vert.

    un chou   **une carotte**   **un champignon**

c) C'est une boisson chaude.

    de la limonade   **un jus d'orange**   **du thé**

d) C'est un dessert.

    un potage   **une glace**   **de l'agneau**

e) C'est un produit laitier.

    du pain   **des fruits de mer**   **un yaourt**

5 marks

29 Circle the correct school subject from the choice of three in each sentence.

a) J'aime *le français / la chimie / l'histoire* **parce je suis forte en sciences.**

b) Ma matière préférée est *la musique / le dessin / les maths* **parce que j'aime jouer du violon.**

c) Je ne peux pas supporter *le français / les maths / l'anglais* **parce que je déteste les pièces de Shakespeare.**

d) J'aime bien *le dessin / le sport / l'informatique* **parce que j'aime travailler avec les ordinateur sur.**

e) *L'histoire / L'anglais / La technologie* **est difficile parce j'oublie facilement les dates.**

5 marks

TOTAL

32

Mixed Test-Style Questions

30 Write at least three things in French that you are going to do in the future in relation to your studies.

....

....

....

6 marks

31 Read Xavier's description of his home town and answer the questions in English.

> Guéret se trouve dans le centre de la France. C'est une petite ville. Il y a un marché, un centre sportif et un musée mais il n'y a pas de théâtre.
>
> Je n'aime pas habiter ici parce qu'il n'y a rien à faire et c'est très ennuyeux.
>
> Limoges est la grande ville la plus proche. Mais Limoges est sale et polluée.
>
> Je préfère la campagne parce que c'est joli et tranquille. À la campagne on peut faire des promenades et du sports comme le cyclisme.

a) Where is Guéret?

....

b) What can you *not* do there?

....

c) Why does Xavier not like living there?

....

d) What does he say about Limoges?

....

e) Why does he like the countryside? Give two reasons.

....

6 marks

32 These verbs take **être** in the perfect tense. In these sentences replace the verb in brackets with the past participle and make it agree if necessary.

Example: **Elle est (aller) chez elle.**

Elle est allée chez elle.

a) **Les trois garçons sont (partir) à deux heures.** _____

b) **Ma sœur est (rester) à la maison.** _____

c) **Philippe est (sortir) avec ses parents.** _____

d) **Julie est (tomber) dans la rue.** _____

e) **Ils sont (rentrer) tard.** _____

f) **Elles sont (retourner) en ville.** _____

6 marks

33 Read what Oscar says and answer the questions below in English.

> **Je m'appelle Oscar et j'habite dans un petit village mais il y a beaucoup de problèmes, par exemple il y a trop de bruit et beaucoup de gens sont au chômage. Pourtant, heureusement il n'y a pas de pollution.**

a) What two problems are there in Oscar's village?

_____

b) What good thing does he mention?

_____

3 marks

34 Translate the following conditional tense phrases into French.

a) I would be rich. _____

b) I would live in France. _____

c) I would buy a big house. _____

3 marks

TOTAL

24

35 Write an appropriate solution in French to each of these energy concerns.

a) **Beaucoup de gens gaspillent l'énergie.**

Il faut _____

b) **Ma mère utilise la voiture trop souvent.**

Il faut _____

c) **J'aime laisser la lumière allumée.**

Il faut _____

☐

6 marks

36 Read Sophie's account of a meal in a restaurant and answer the questions in English.

> **Pour mon anniversaire on est allé dans un restaurant assez cher pas loin de chez nous. On a très bien mangé (j'ai choisi le poulet rôti avec des petits pois et une salade) mais le service n'était pas rapide – on a dû attendre une heure pour le dessert. Quand mon dessert est enfin arrivé, il était froid.**

a) Why did Sophie go to the restaurant?

_____

b) Where was the restaurant?

_____

c) What did she order?

_____

d) What does she say about the service?

_____

e) What was wrong with her dessert?

_____

☐

5 marks

Total

☐

11

37 Read what Ann-Sophie says about her job and answer the questions in English.

> Je suis avocate et normalement je travaille tous les jours sauf le dimanche. Pour être avocat il faut être travailleuse et on doit aimer travailler seule ou en équipe. Il y a beaucoup d'avantages de mon travail, par exemple c'est varié et c'est bien payé, mais c'est aussi très difficile et très stressant. Quand j'étais jeune j'étais vraiment intéressée par la justice donc j'ai voulu toujours être avocate et heureusement j'adore mon boulot!

a) When does Ann-Sophie work?

....

b) What traits must you have in order to be a good lawyer?

....

c) What are the advantages of Ann-Sophie's job?

....

d) What are the disadvantages?

....

e) What was Ann-Sophie interested in when she was young?

....

8 marks

38 Put the following future tense sentences into French.

a) I will eat my dinner in the dining room.

....

b) He will buy a t-shirt with his pocket money.

....

c) They will go to the museum with the school.

....

d) We will be too tired.

....

4 marks

TOTAL

12

Mixed Test-Style Questions

39 Correct the adjectives in this paragraph.

Au collège je porte une beau _____ **veste noir** _____ **avec une**

jupe joli _____ **. On peut porter une chemise blanc** _____ **ou bleue**

et il faut porter une cravate rouges _____ **. Je n'aime pas les chaussures**

noires parce qu'elles sont vraiment ennuyeux _____ **.**

6 marks

40 Make up five complex sentences using the phrases below and either **quand** (when) or **si** (if).

il fait beau	je vais à la plage	normalement
il fait froid	je reste à l'hôtel	d'habitude
il y a du soleil	je me promène	le matin
il pleut	je vais à la piscine	le soir
j'ai le temps	je fais des courses	l'après-midi

En vacances...

_____

_____

_____

_____

5 marks

41 Make five sentences, choosing a word from each list. Remember to change the adjective endings.

Je trouve que	ma sœur	tout le temps	très	amusant
Je pense que	mon frère	parfois	un peu	barbant
Selon moi	ma meilleure copine	ne…jamais	vraiment	bête
À mon avis	mon meilleur copain	ne…pas	trop	ennuyeux

_____

_____

_____

5 marks

Total

16

Mix it Up

42 Describe your favourite singer/actor or a person you admire using the key phrases below.
Remember to change your adjective endings to agree with the noun they describe.

s'appelle	les cheveux	parce que/car/puisque
il/elle a…ans	les yeux	j'aime/ j'adore/j'admire
il/elle a	anglais/américain/français	je trouve que/je pense que
il/elle est	grand/petit/talentueux/ bon	chanteur/ acteur/ musicien/athlète

....
....
....
....

5 marks

43 Draw a line to match the items of food with the correct type of cuisine.

le curry	la cuisine américaine
les spaghettis à la bolognaise	la cuisine japonaise
le sushi	la cuisine espagnole
les tapas	la cuisine italienne
le hamburger	la cuisine indienne
le haggis	la cuisine écossaise

6 marks

TOTAL

11

Mixed Test-Style Questions

44 Read Assiom's description of his school in Togo in Africa and answer the questions below with true or false.

> **Au Togo, les élèves portent un uniforme d'une même couleur. A mon école, par exemple, c'est le vert. Les filles doivent porter une robe verte et les garçons une chemise verte avec un bermuda vert. Les cours ont lieu le matin de 7h à 12h et il y a une quarantaine d'élèves dans ma classe. Il n'y a pas de cours l'après-midi parce qu'il fait trop chaud. Mes matières sont: le français, l'anglais, les maths, l'histoire-géo, l'allemand et l'économie générale. J'aime mon école parce que les élèves travaillent dur et le professeur est très gentil.**

a) All the pupils in Assiom's school wear green clothes. _____

b) There are about thirty pupils in his class. _____

c) There are only lessons in the morning. _____

d) This is due to the heat. _____

4 marks

45 Read Thomas's description of his local area and answer the questions in English.

> **J'habite une petite ville qui s'appelle Ballon. Il y a beaucoup de choses pour les touristes dans ma région. Près de Ballon il y a les ruines d'un château. Au centre-ville il y a une belle église du quinzième siècle. Je voudrais habiter dans la même ville que ma cousine parce qu'il y a beaucoup de choses à faire pour les adolescents : par exemple, aller au cinéma et faire les magasins avec ses amis. Il y a aussi un grand complexe sportif. Je n'aime pas la ville où j'habite parce qu'il n'y a pas beaucoup à faire, il n'y a pas de piscine, ni de centre commercial.**

a) What two things can tourists visit in Thomas' region?

_____

b) Where would he like to live?

6 marks

_____

Total

c) Name three things teenagers can do there.

_____

10

Answers

Family (pages 148–149)

1. a) Karima
   b) Alexandre
   c) Jean
   d) Chloé
   e) Pauline [5]

2. a) Mon anniversaire c'est le six décembre.
   b) Mon anniversaire c'est le cinq juin. [2]

3. a) Sébastien
   b) Sébastien
   c) Ophélie and Laure
   d) Myriam [4]

4. a) I have brown, long, straight hair (3). I have blue eyes (1) and I am very tall (2).
   b) I am quite small (2) and I have brown eyes (1). I have black, short hair (2).
   c) We are twin boys (2). We have (1) blond, straight, very short (3) hair.
   d) I have a little, black (2) cat (1). [20]

5. a) 13 the day of the month Marcel was born
   b) 14 Marcel's age
   c) 40 Isabelle's mum's age
   d) 45 Isabelle's dad's age
   e) 10 Isabelle's brothers' age [5]

House and Home (pages 150–151)

1. a) J'habite dans le nord de la France.
      I live in the north of France.
   b) Ma maison se trouve au centre-ville.
      My house is located in the town centre.
   c) Chez nous il y a dix pièces. At home there are ten rooms.
   d) Nous n'avons pas de jardin. We don't have a garden.
   e) Notre maison a deux étages et un grenier.
      Our house has two floors and an attic.
   f) Il y a trois chambres au premier étage.
      There are three bedrooms on the first floor.

   g) Ma chambre est à côté de la chambre de mes parents.
      My bedroom is next to my parents' bedroom.
   h) Ma chambre est (très) petite mais très jolie.
      My bedroom is (very) small but very pretty.
   i) Il y a beaucoup de choses dans ma chambre.
      There are lots of things in my bedroom.
   j) Je n'ai pas de télévision dans ma chambre.
      I don't have a television in my bedroom. [10]

2. a) ma
   b) ma
   c) mon; mon
   d) mes; mon
   e) ma
   f) mes
   g) ma
   h) mon [10]

3. Où habites-tu? J'habite en Corse, près de la mer.
   Tu habites loin de la mer? Non, assez près, à environ cinq minutes.
   Tu aimes ta ville? Oui, parce que mes amis y habitent aussi.
   Comment est ta maison? Elle est assez petite.
   Tu as un jardin? Oui, et il est très grand.
   Tu aides tes parents à la maison? Oui, je fais souvent le ménage.
   Qu'est-ce qu'il y a dans ta chambre? Il y a mon lit et mon armoire.
   Tu as un ordinateur dans ta chambre? Non, mais nous avons un ordinateur dans le salon. [8]

Food and Drink (pages 152–153)

1. a) 4 euros
   b) 7 euros
   c) 8 euros
   d) 3 euros
   e) 1 euro
   f) 2 euros [6]

2. a) omelette aux champignons
   b) sandwich au fromage
   c) tarte à la fraise
   d) soupe à l'oignon
   e) steak-frites [5]

3. Moi, je préfère la cuisine italienne parce
   que j'aime les pâtes et les pizzas. J'adore les
   spaghettis à la bolognaise. Comme dessert,
   j'aime les glaces. D'habitude, je bois du jus
   d'orange parce que je n'aime pas tellement les
   boissons gazeuses, comme la limonade. Je prends
   quelquefois une boisson chaude, du café au lait,
   par exemple. [6]

4. a) P
   b) P
   c) N
   d) P / N
   e) P
   f) N
   g) P / N
   h) N [8]

Sport and Health (pages 154–155)

1. Le weekend, j'aime aller à la piscine, où je fais de
   la natation.
   Le weekend, j'aime faire de l'équitation. J'aime les
   chevaux.
   Je fais souvent du vélo. J'adore le cyclisme.
   J'adore les sports nautiques comme la voile.
   J'aime regarder le foot. Je vais souvent au stade.
   J'aime le patinage mais je tombe souvent. [6]

2. a) N
   b) P / N
   c) N
   d) P
   e) P / N
   f) P
   g) N
   h) P [8]

3. a) G
   b) D
   c) A
   d) E
   e) C
   f) B
   g) F [7]

4. a) sportif
   b) violent
   c) natation
   d) mauvais; cancer
   e) forme; légumes [7]

School and Education (pages 156–157)

1. a) G
   b) C
   c) B
   d) D
   e) A
   f) E [6]

2. a) ennuyeux
   b) de copains
   c) trop difficile
   d) sympas
   e) nulle
   f) livres [6]

3. a) True
   b) True
   c) True
   d) False
   e) True
   f) False [6]

4. a) Arthur
   b) Claire
   c) Salma
   d) Claire
   e) Arthur
   f) Arthur
   g) Salma
   h) Claire [8]

Future Plans (pages 158–159)

1. après   afterwards
   l'année prochaine   next year
   puis   then / next

à l'avenir   in the future

d'abord   first of all

dans trois ans   in three years   **[6]**

2. avocate; coiffeuse; directrice; infirmière;
   traductrice   **[5]**

3. **a)** quitter

   b) continuer

   c) aller

   d) voyager

   e) habiter

   f) avoir   **[6]**

4. **a)** Je dois être motivé. I must be motivated.

   b) Il faut coopérer avec ses collègues. You must /
   have to cooperate with colleagues.

   c) Je peux communiquer mes idées. I can
   communicate my ideas.   **[6]**

5. **a)** translator **(1)**

   b) She can work alone and in a team. **(2)**

   c) communicate with lots of people **(1)**

   d) It is interesting and well paid. **(2)**

   e) She would like to work abroad **(1)** because it is
   rewarding **(1)** and stimulating **(1)**.   **[9]**

Leisure, Free Time and Media (pages 160–161)

1. **a)** 9:15

   b) 12:00

   c) 8:45

   d) 20:00

   e) 13:30   **[5]**

2. Tu veux aller au concert de Stromae avec nous?
   Tu veux aller à la patinoire ce soir?
   Tu veux venir au parc Astérix avec nous?
   On y va à dix heures?
   On va à la piscine à neuf heures demain?   **[5]**

3. **a)** au + a masculine place or à la + feminine
   place.

   b) any day such as lundi, mardi, etc – no 'on'.

   c) a time such as dix heures or dix heures et
   demie.

   d) choose a preposition to indicate where exactly

   e) a time such as dix heures or dix heures
   et demie.   **[5]**

4. **a)** On va au cinéma à neuf heures et demie.

   b) On va à la piscine à dix heures.

   c) On va au restaurant à dix-huit heures.

   d) On va au concert à vingt-et-une heures / neuf
   heures du soir.

   e) On va au centre commercial à quatorze heures /
   deux heures de l'après-midi.   **[10]**

5. g ; d ; b ; e ; f ; a or c ; a or c   **[7]**

TV and Technology (pages 162–163)

1. **a)** un dessin animé – a cartoon

   b) une série – a series

   c) une comédie – a comedy

   d) la météo – the weather

   e) les infos – the news   **[10]**

2. de temps en temps   from time to time

   le weekend   at the weekend

   rarement   rarely

   souvent   often

   tous les jours   everyday

   une / deux fois par semaine once / twice
   a week   **[6]**

3. **a)** même si

   b) de temps en temps

   c) assez   **[3]**

4. Many answers are possible. For example:
   Je regarde les émissions de sport tous les jours
   car elles sont vraiment intéressantes. (**1 mark**
   each for an appropriate frequency word,
   connective, intensifier and opinion: total
   4 marks)

5. **a)** She doesn't like it.

   b) twice a week

   c) They are really funny.

   d) Her brother **(1)**, sometimes **(1)**.   **[5]**

6. There is no right answer to this question, but here
   are some examples of advantages:
   Ça m'aide à me détendre.
   On peut s'échapper de la vie quotidienne.
   C'est déstressant.
   On peut regarder la télé en famille
   Il est moins cher que sortir.

Ça m'aide à communiquer avec mes amis.

C'est plus facile de changer des projets.

On peut communiquer plus facilement.

On peut se tenir au courant.

Je me sens plus en sécurité.

(**1 mark** for each up to a maximum of **5 marks**)

Shopping and Money (pages 164–165)

1. 20 Euros **(1)**, per month **(1)**

2. **a)** cotton

   b) leather

   c) wool [3]

3. **a)** une jupe bleue (The colour comes after the noun.)

   b) un pantalon gris (The colour needs a masculine spelling.)

   c) une cravate jaune (If the colour already ends in an e there is no need to add another.)

   d) un pull noir (The colour comes after the noun.)

   e) une chemise violette (The colour needs a feminine ending.)

   f) des chaussures marron (Marron never changes its spelling.) [6]

4. **a)** une cravate

   b) un pull

   c) une robe

   d) un tee-shirt [4]

5. **a)** Her dad

   b) 40 Euros **(1)**, per month **(1)**

   c) CDs **(1)**, makeup **(1)**

   d) Saves it **(1)**, to buy a bike **(1)** [7]

6. Chloé [1]

7. Je reçois vingt euros par semaine **(1)** car je garde mon petit frère **(1)**. Avec mon argent de poche j'achète des vêtements **(1)** et je fais des économies. [3]

Where I Live (pages 166–167)

1. **a)** le centre de recyclage

   b) la gare

   c) un centre commercial

   d) une banque

   e) un jardin public

   f) le centre de loisirs [6]

2. **a)** A

   b) C

   c) G

   d) F

   e) B [5]

3. **a)** Old town, see the churches, walk

   b) Park, see the roses, bus [6]

4. **a)** north west France

   b) shopping centre, sports centre, pool, stadium, theatre, cinema, library (any two for **two marks**)

   c) lots to do / lively

   d) Cathedral, museums, old town (any two for **two marks**)

   e) Doesn't like it, too quiet, nothing to do, transport not frequent (any two for **two marks**) [8]

Holidays (pages 168–169)

1. une semaine et demie — one and a half weeks

   deux semaines — two weeks

   quinze jours — a fortnight

   un mois — one month

   dix jours — ten days [5]

2. **a)** Normalement je vais à Paris avec ma famille pour une semaine.

   b) Normalement je vais au Canada avec mes parents pour un mois.

   c) Normalement je vais à Lyon avec mes grands-parents pour deux semaines.

   d) Normalement je vais en Angleterre avec ma mère pour dix jours.

   e) Normalement je vais en Espagne avec mon père pour une semaine. [15]

3. **a)** B

   b) A

   c) D

   d) C [4]

4. **a)** Je voudrais une chambre pour deux nuits.

   b) Je voudrais une chambre avec deux lits.

   c) Vous avez / Avez-vous une chambre avec balcon?

   d) Il y a un restaurant? Est-ce qu'il y a un restaurant?

   e) Il y a un ascenseur dans l'hôtel? Est-ce qu'il y a un ascenseur dans l'hôtel?

f) Il y a une piscine? Est-ce qu'il y a une piscine?

g) Ma chambre est sale.

h) La télévision ne marche pas.

i) La douche est cassée (agreement of cassé with douche, which is feminine). **[9]**

Global Issues (pages 170–171)

1.

le changement climatique	climate change
la déforestation	deforestation
l'énergie nucléaire	nuclear energy
les inondations	floods
les marées noires	oil slicks
le recyclage	recycling
la surpêche	over-fishing **[7]**

2. a) You must / it is necessary to.

b) It is always followed by an infinitive. **[2]**

3. a) Throw!

b) Avoid!

c) Reduce!

d) Support!

e) Save! **[5]**

4. Students' own answers. **[2]**

5. a) Concern: Poverty

Solution: Give to charity

b) Concern: Deforestation

Solution: Recycle paper

c) Concern: Hunger

Solution: Organise events

d) Concern: Endangered species

Solution: Protecting animals **[8]**

6. Students' own answers. **[2]**

Gender and Plurals (page 172)

1. a) une

b) une

c) une

d) un

e) un

f) un

g) une

h) un

i) un

j) une **[10]**

2. a) des bateaux

b) des tapis

c) des chapeaux

d) des chevaux

e) des souris

f) des journaux

g) des tables

h) des nez

i) des châteaux

j) des animaux **[10]**

3. a) un

b) le

c) la

d) des

e) de

f) un

g) des

h) les

i) un

j) un

k) les

l) un **[12]**

Adjectives (page 173)

1. petit; grand; rouge; sympa; paresseux; français **[6]**

2. a) grande (feminine)

b) gros (masculine)

c) dégoûtants (masculine plural)

d) ancien (masculine)

e) hivernale (feminine) **[5]**

3. a) petites (feminine plural)

b) grande (feminine)

c) noirs (masculine plural)

d) blonde (feminine)

e) sportives (feminine plural)

f) paresseuses (feminine plural)

g) plus âgé que (masculine)

h) plus grande (feminine)

i) plus petite (feminine)

j) la meilleure (feminine) **[10]**

Avoir and Être (page 174)

1. Je suis français.

Paris est la capitale de la France.

Aurélie Joly et Myriam Soumaré sont des athlètes.

Tu es parisien?

Nous sommes originaires de la Guadeloupe.   **[5]**

2. a) suis; avons; a

   b) es; est

   c) sont

   d) est; sommes; ai

   e) est; a

   f) est   **[12]**

3. a) J'ai 14 ans et ma sœur a 16 ans.

   b) Quel âge a ta sœur?

   c) Mon ami a le même âge que moi.

   d) Tu as soif?

   e) J'ai très faim.   **[5]**

ER, IR and RE Verbs (page 175)

1.

to eat	manger
to sing	chanter
to like	aimer
to live	habiter
to finish	finir
to choose	choisir
to wait	attendre
to sell	vendre **[8]**

2.

	je	tu	il/elle	nous	vous	ils/elles
-ER verbs	-e	-es	-e	-ons	-ez	-ent
-IR verbs	-is	-is	-it	-issons	-issez	-issent
-RE verbs	-s	-s	nothing	-ons	-ez	-ent

[12]

3. a) fête

   b) aime

   c) habitons

   d) dansons

   e) aime

   f) mangent -déteste

   g) finit

   h) attendent

   i) vendez   **[10]**

Modal Verbs (page 176)

1. a) Je veux…   I want to go to town.

   b) Ils doivent…   They must buy presents.

   c) Nous ne   We can't go to the
      pouvons pas…   cinema.

   d) Fatima doit…   Fatima must do her maths
                  homework.

   e) Vous voulez…   Do you want to
                  come with us?   **[10]**

2. a) veux

   b) peux

   c) doit

   d) peux

   e) veulent

   f) devons

   g) pouvez   **[7]**

3. a) Pouvez-vous (peux-tu) venir chez moi
      (à ma maison)?

   b) Je veux sortir samedi soir.

   c) Elle doit travailler dur.

   d) Les ami(e)s peuvent faire du vélo.

   e) Nous voulons acheter des cadeaux.   **[5]**

Faire, Aller and the Immediate Future (page 177)

1. a) Mon frère va regarder la télé.

   b) Les deux filles vont danser.

   c) Tu vas écouter de la musique?

   d) Je vais jouer au foot dans le jardin.

   e) Nous allons sortir ensemble.   **[5]**

2. a) Nous faisons

   b) Vous faites

   c) Ils font

   d) Elles font   **[4]**

3. a) Les filles vont au théâtre.

   b) Samedi, nous allons au parc d'attractions.

   c) Je ne vais jamais au marché.

   d) Est-ce que vous allez avec votre frère?

   e) Tu vas aux magasins?

   f) Grégoire va au stade.   **[6]**

Imperative and Reflexive Verbs (page 178)

1. a) Close the door!
   b) Let's eat now.
   c) Don't speak!
   d) Play with your sister!
   e) Go to the dentist!
   f) Let's listen to music!
   g) Don't go in the living room!
   h) Leave / go out immediately! **[8]**

2. a) Les enfants se lèvent quand le professeur entre dans la salle de classe.
   b) À quelle heure est-ce que tu te couches?
   c) Tous les jours, nous nous lavons dans la salle de bains.
   d) Juliette s'habille dans sa chambre. Elle met une jupe, un pull et un chemisier.
   e) Avant de manger, je me lave les mains. **[5]**

3. a) Je me réveille à sept heures.
   b) Il se lève à sept heures et quart.
   c) Tu te laves (vous vous lavez) dans la salle de bains.
   d) Elle s'habille dans sa chambre.
   e) Ils / elles se relaxent / se réposent dans le salon.
   f) Je me couche à dix heures. **[6]**

Perfect Tense (page 179)

1. a) I went shopping on Saturday afternoon.
   b) We watched a DVD together.
   c) Did you see the film? / Have you seen the film?
   d) I went out with my friends.
   e) She stayed at home.
   f) He answered my question.
   g) Have you chosen / did you choose a book? **[7]**

2. a) J'ai mangé un sandwich au fromage.
   b) Julie a joué de la guitare.
   c) Nous avons écouté de la musique.
   d) Tu as fini tes devoirs?
   e) Vous avez nagé dans la mer?
   f) Elle est allée au supermarché.
   g) Les deux amis sont arrivés à deux heures.
   h) J'ai fait du ski nautique. **[8]**

3. a) Je suis allé(e) au jardin public / parc.
   b) Nous avons vu le film.
   c) Il n'a pas mangé le gâteau.
   d) Elle est entrée dans la maison.
   e) Tu as parlé / vous avez parlé à son père.
   f) Les trois filles sont restées dans la salle de classe.
   g) J'ai acheté des chaussures.
   h) Il est arrivé à la gare. **[8]**

Future Tense (page 180)

1. a) jouaient – it is imperfect tense, the rest are future tense.
   b) mangeons – it is present tense, the rest are future tense.
   c) irait – it is conditional tense, the rest are future tense.
   d) vendrez – it is future tense, the rest are present tense. **[4]**

2.

Infinitive	Stem	Future tense
visiter	visiter	il visitera
écouter	écouter	tu écouteras
choisir	choisir	je choisirai
perdre	perdr	ils perdront
être	ser	nous serons
avoir	aur	vous aurez

[10]

3. a) mangeras should be mangerai
   b) attendons should be attendrons
   c) irai should be ira
   d) visiterent should be visiteront **[4]**

Pronouns (page 181)

1. a) emphatic pronoun (elle is being used to highlight the subject of the sentence)
   b) direct object pronoun (le / la is being used to replace the object of the verb)
   c) subject pronoun (vous is the subject of the verb)
   d) indirect object pronoun (leur is being used to replace the object of the verb and in this case the verb requires the object be preceded by the word à) **[4]**

2. a) y

    b) en

    c) en

    d) y   **[4]**

3. a) Il les adore.

    b) Ils la chantent.

    c) Elle le regarde.   **[6]**

    (**6 marks**, 1 mark for each correct pronoun in the correct position)

4. a) se

    b) te

    c) m'

    d) se

    e) nous   **[5]**

Imperfect Tense (page 182)

1. Perfect tense: a single completed action in the past   **[1]**

Imperfect tense: something you used to do or a repeated action in the past or a description of the past (e.g. opinion/ weather)   **[3]**

2. (10 marks, 1 mark for each correct answer)

Infinitive	Stem	Imperfect tense
finir	finiss	je finissais
aller	all	tu allais
vendre	vend	il vendait
dormir	dorm	nous dormions
perdre	perd	vous perdiez
parler	parl	elles parlaient

3. a) Je jouais au foot.

    b) Il visitait l'exposition tous les jours.

    c) Nous allions au parc le weekend.

    d) Vous étiez drôle.   **[4]**

Conditional Tense and Passive Voice (page 183)

1. a) j'irais

    b) je mangerais

    c) elle achéterait   **[3]**

2. a) Active

    b) Passive

    c) Passive

    d) Active   **[4]**

3. a) Le magazine est acheté par Luc.

    b) La soupe à été mangée par Zara.

    c) Le mannequin sera dessiné par Thomas.

    d) Les chansons sont chantées par la chorale.   **[4]**

4. a) She was seen.

    b) He is liked by everyone.

    c) He will be punished.   **[6]**

    (**6 marks**: 1 for each correct translation of vocabulary, 1 for correct translation of passive voice)

Mixed Test-Style Questions (pages 184–203)

1. Il est huit heures trente.   8.30

Il est dix-neuf heures.   19.00

Il est sept heures.   7.00

Il est deux heures moins le quart.   1.45

Il est minuit.   0.00

Il est quatorze heures quinze.   14.15   **[6]**

2. a) A

    b) D

    c) C

    d) B   **[4]**

3. a) Olivier

    b) Enzo

    c) 14th July

    d) 6th January

    e) The person who gets the feve.

    f) chocolate eggs   **[6]**

4. a) one dog and two cats

    b) a little white dog

    c) three gold fish

    d) two horses

    e) none   **[5]**

5. a) blue

    b) six

    c) seven

    d) twelve

    e) blue

    f) green   **[6]**

6. a) Guadeloupe

    b) Her family lives there.

    c) French and Creole

    d) her mum, step dad and step brother

    e) August

f) three weeks

g) in a hotel

h) go to the beach

i) every summer

j) the food **[10]**

7. a) Je m'appelle Sébastien. Je suis grand. J'ai les yeux bleus et j'ai les cheveux blonds. **[4]**

b) Je m'appelle Karima. Je suis petite. J'ai les yeux marron et j'ai les cheveux longs. **[4]**

8. Reporter: Bonjour, Pierre. Ça va?

Pierre: Oui, très bien, merci.

Reporter: Quelle est la date de ton anniversaire?

Pierre: Je suis né le 20 mars.

Reporter: Tu as quel âge?

Pierre: C'est un secret!

Reporter: Tu as des frères et des sœurs?

Pierre: Oui, un frère et une sœur.

Reporter: Où habites-tu?

Pierre: J'habite en France mais mes parents viennent de la Martinique.

Reporter: Tu parles créole?

Pierre: Non, malheureusement!

Reporter: Merci, Pierre.

Pierre: De rien! **[6]**

9. a) 30/9

b) 2/5

c) 1/8

d) 13/3

e) 12/1 **[5]**

10. a) To the ice rink.

b) Tomorrow **(1)** at 2pm / 14:00 **(1)**

c) He must stay at home with his sister.

d) on foot

e) to go later

f) At Benjamin's house **(1)** at 3pm / 15:00 **(1)** **[7]**

11. Bonjour! Hello!

Salut! Hi!

Bonne journée! Have a good day!

A bientôt! See you soon!

Au revoir! Goodbye!

Bon anniversaire! Happy birthday!

Bonne nuit! Good night!

Bonsoir! Good evening! **[8]**

12. a) Where is the swimming pool?

b) Where is the restaurant?

c) Is there a lift?

d) Is there a shower in the room? **[4]**

13. a) Isabelle

b) Lucie

c) Laure

d) Laure **[4]**

14. a) children

b) Sophie, a little girl

c) In a castle, in France

d) Sophie's friends

e) Funny or curious or adventurous

f) naughty or mischievous

g) Her cousin, Paul **[7]**

15. à la mode fashionable / trendy

à pois polka dotted

cool cool

demodé(e) old-fashioned

écossais(e) tartan

moche ugly

rayé stripy **[7]**

16. a) fois

b) mais; vraiment

c) regarder

d) car; émouvants

e) jamais **[7]**

17. a) la natation

b) le tennis

c) le ski

d) le football

e) le rugby **[5]**

18. a) relaxing, good for the heart, a way to make new friends

b) swimming

c) causes cancer; endangers others

d) reads a book; listens to music

e) not going to drink too many fizzy drinks because it's bad for your health **[10]**

19. à mon avis in my opinion

en ce qui me concerne as far as I'm concerned

je pense que   I think that

je crois que   I believe that   **[4]**

20. e.g. J'achète des vêtements. Je fais des économies.

   (**4 marks**, up to 2 marks per answer depending on length)

21. **a)** les haricots verts

   b) les pommes

   c) du chocolat

   d) la soupe

   e) les fromages   **[5]**

22. **a)** Je n'aime pas la musique parce que le professeur est strict.

   b) Ma matière préférée est le dessin parce que c'est facile.

   c) Je déteste les sciences, surtout la physique.

   d) Les cours commencent à huit heures et demie.

   e) À la pause-déjeuner, je mange à la cantine avec mes ami(e)s.

   f) Je vais à l'école en voiture.

   g) Les cours finissent à trois heures et demie.

   h) Il est interdit de parler en classe.   **[8]**

23. **a)** False

   b) True

   c) False

   d) True

   e) False

   f) False   **[6]**

24. **a)** le centre commercial

   b) musée

   c) le stade

   d) la piscine

   e) le jardin public   **[5]**

25. **a)** A

   b) D

   c) D

   d) A

   e) D

   f) D

   g) A

   h) A

   i) A

   j) D   **[10]**

26. e.g. Au college je porte un pull bleu et une chemise blanche avec un pantalon noir.

   (**6 marks**: 1 mark for each item, 1 for each description)   **[6]**

27. **a)** the planet

   b) over-fishing; cruelty; deforestation **(3)**

   c) destruction of habitats

   d) protect animals   **[6]**

28. **a)** une fraise

   b) un chou

   c) du thé

   d) une glace

   e) un yaourt   **[5]**

29. **a)** la chimie

   b) la musique

   c) l'anglais

   d) l'informatique

   e) l'histoire   **[5]**

30. **6 marks**: up to 2 marks per future intention depending on length of answer.

31. **a)** in the middle / centre of France

   b) go to the theatre

   c) It's boring / nothing to do

   d) It's dirty and polluted and is the nearest city.

   e) go walking, do sports like cycling, it is pretty, it is quiet (any two for **two marks**).   **[6]**

32. **a)** sont partis

   b) est restée

   c) est sorti

   d) est tombée

   e) sont rentrés

   f) sont retournées   **[6]**

33. **a)** too much noise **(1)**, unemployment **(1)**

   b) no pollution   **[3]**

34. **a)** Je serais riche.

   b) J'habiterais en France.

   c) J'achèterais une grande maison.   **[3]**

35. **a)** e.g. Il faut économiser l'énergie.

   b) e.g. Il faut utiliser les transports en commun.

   c) e.g. Il faut éteindre la lumière quand on quitte la pièce.   **[6]**

36. **a)** for her birthday

   b) not far from where she lives

c) (roast) chicken, peas and salad

d) slow / not quick

e) it was cold [5]

37. a) Every day except Sunday **(1)**

b) Hard working, like working alone or in a team **(2)**

c) Varied, well-paid **(2)**

d) Hard/difficult, stressful **(2)**

e) Justice **(1)** [8]

38. a) Je mangerai mon dîner dans la salle à manger.

b) Il achètera un t-shirt avec son argent de poche.

c) Ils iront au musée avec le collège.

d) Nous serons trop fatigués. [4]

39. Au collège je porte une **belle (1)** veste **noire (1)** avec une **jolie (1)** jupe. On peut porter une chemise **blanche (1)** ou bleue et il faut porter une cravate **rouge (1)**. Je n'aime pas les chaussures noires parce qu'elles sont vraiment **ennuyeuses (1)**. [6]

40. Example: En vacances, s'il fait beau, d'habitude je me promène. (On holiday if the weather is nice I usually go for a walk.) [5]

41. Example: Je pense que ma sœur **est** parfois très ennuy**euse**. (I think that my sister is sometimes very boring.) [5]

42. Example: Mon acteur préféré s'appelle Vincent Cassel. Il a les cheveux et les yeux marron. Vicent Cassel est un acteur français et je trouve qu'il est très bon. Je pense qu'il a environ 45 ans. [5]

43.
le curry	la cuisine indienne
les spaghettis à la bolognaise	la cuisine italienne
le sushi	la cuisine japonaise
les tapas	la cuisine espagnole
le hamburger	la cuisine américaine
le haggis	la cuisine écossaise [6]

44. a) True

b) False

c) True

d) True [4]

45. a) the castle **(1)** and the church **(1)**

b) where his cousin lives

c) go to the cinema **(1)**, go shopping **(1)**, go to the sports centre **(1)** [6]

Revision Tips

Rethink Revision

Have you ever taken part in a quiz and thought *'I know this!'*, but no matter how hard you scrabbled around in your brain you just couldn't come up with the answer?

It's very frustrating when this happens, but in a fun situation it doesn't really matter. However, in tests and assessments, it is essential that you can recall the relevant information when you need to.

Most students think that revision is about making sure you **know** *stuff*, but it is also about being confident that you can **retain** that *stuff* over time and **recall** it when needed.

Revision that Really Works

Experts have found that there are two techniques that help with *all* of these things and consistently produce better results in tests and exams compared to other revision techniques.

Applying these techniques to your KS3 revision will ensure you get better results in tests and assessments and will have all the relevant knowledge at your fingertips when you start studying for your GCSEs.

It really isn't rocket science either – you simply need to:

* **test yourself** on each topic as many times as possible
* **leave a gap** between the test sessions.

It is most effective if you leave a good period of time between the test sessions, e.g. between a week and a month. The idea is that just as you start to forget the information, you force yourself to recall it again, keeping it fresh in your mind.

Three Essential Revision Tips

1 Use Your Time Wisely
* Allow yourself plenty of time
* Try to start revising six months before tests and assessments – it's more effective and less stressful
* Your revision time is precious so use it wisely – using the techniques described on this page will ensure you revise effectively and efficiently and get the best results
* Don't waste time re-reading the same information over and over again – it's time-consuming and not effective!

2 Make a Plan
* Identify all the topics you need to revise (this Complete Revision & Practice book will help you)
* Plan at least five sessions for each topic
* A one-hour session should be ample to test yourself on the key ideas for a topic
* Spread out the practice sessions for each topic – the optimum time to leave between each session is about one month but, if this isn't possible, just make the gaps as big as realistically possible.

3 Test Yourself
* Methods for testing yourself include: quizzes, practice questions, flashcards, past-papers, explaining a topic to someone else, etc.
* This Complete Revision & Practice book gives you seven practice test opportunities per topic
* Don't worry if you get an answer wrong – provided you check what the right answer is, you are more likely to get the same or similar questions right in future!

Visit our website to download your free flashcards, for more information about the benefits of these revision techniques and for further guidance on how to plan ahead and make them work for you.

www.collins.co.uk/collinsks3revision